P9-DFW-847
IBRAHIM MOUSTAFA
RETRO ACTIVE
with BRAD SIMPSON
& HASSAN OTSMANE-ELHAOU
HUMANOIDS

IBRAHIM MOUSTAFA
Writer & Artist

BRAD SIMPSON
Color Artist

HASSAN OTSMANE-ELHAOU
Letterer

IBRAHIM MOUSTAFA
Cover

ROB LEVIN
Editor

JERRY FRISSEN
Senior Art Director

MARK WAID
Publisher

Rights and Licensing - licensing@humanoids.com
Press and Social Media - pr@humanoids.com

RETROACTIVE. First Printing. This book is a publication of Humanoids, Inc. 8033 Sunset Blvd. #628, Los Angeles, CA 90046.

Library of Congress Control Number: 2021945734

For all of us who rarely see people like ourselves reflected in fiction.
-Ibrahim

PRAISE FOR ***RETROACTIVE***:

"A rock-solid time-travel thriller with impeccable action sequences and real human emotions."
—Steve Lieber (*Whiteout, Superman's Pal Jimmy Olsen*)

"RetroActive *is a mile a minute thrill ride by a cartoonist at the top of their game. Clear, concise and action-packed storytelling make this a great read with some serious depth. Ibrahim keeps the reader guessing up until the very end. I couldn't put it down."*
—Michael Walsh (*The Silver Coin, Comeback*)

"Tackling the morality and responsibility involved with time-traveling, RetroActive *is a fast-paced time travel story that will have you guessing at every time jump. I devoured this story in one sitting. Ibrahim Moustafa and the team have crafted a suspenseful story with gorgeous artwork that you won't be able to put down."*
—Stephanie Phillips (*Harley Quinn, The Butcher of Paris*)

"Breathlessly cinematic. Forget three-dimensional: this is a four-dimensional sci-fi spy epic the likes of which we haven't seen in decades—if ever."
—Phil Nobile, Jr. (*Editor-in-Chief, Fangoria*)

"Tightly wound MI6-style espionage with mind-bendingly dangerous time travel. Auteur Ibrahim Moustafa is quickly carving out his own comics niche with one slick, sci-fi action gem after another. Retroactive *is a rush. I wish I could travel back in time and experience it fresh all over again."*
—Tony Fleecs (*Stray Dogs, Time Shopper*)

INTRODUCTION

Ibrahim Moustafa is merciless.

Not with you, dear reader, but with himself. There are a lot of talented writer/artists in comics, a scary number in fact, all with scary talent, just like Ibrahim. But there are very few with the discipline needed to create a work like the book you now hold.

I write and draw comics for a living myself, and I know from experience that the talent that landed me this career can also be a deadly trap. Talent is fun. Too fun. From the moment you recognize you have it, to the hard work of building it, to the joyous exercise of it, talent provides one of the most fulfilling experiences of an artist's life. That's why it's so dangerous. You can fall in love with your own skill to the point of distraction. You can ride your talent straight into every bad habit lying in wait for a cartoonist. You can become a parody of yourself, refining and purifying that same solitary nugget of talent until it's a featureless orb in which the only thing visible is your own reflection.

But not Ibrahim.

Ibrahim is merciless with himself. To create a story as imaginative, compelling, personal, and thrilling as RetroActive, he had to be. For one thing, there's THE BIG IDEA, or the "high concept" as folks in the entertainment business call it. The big idea at the center of this book is a doozy, and it would be easy to fall into the trap of explaining its every contour and cranny to the reader. Why not show off such a great idea? Because a great idea doesn't always make for a great story.

Ibrahim knows when to stop showing off his conceptual bona fides and start displaying his chops as a storyteller. From the opening pages of this stunning graphic novel, you can tell Ibrahim knows when to let the action do the talking. And more importantly, he knows when to let us into the lives of the people behind that action so we actually care about the choices they make. His knack for jumping from small humanizing details to epic spectacle then back to deftly crafted plot twists is downright uncanny.

And he's not shy about dropping in some nifty bits of formal experimentation when you least expect it but most need it. He's ably abetted in all this by the simpatico comic-crafting skills of colorist Brad Simpson and letterer Hassan Otsmane-Elhaou, both somehow able to keep pace with Ibrahim's roaring engine of creativity.

In short, Ibrahim took what could have been a sprawling, overly technical exercise in hard science fiction and forged it into a finely honed, taut thriller with devastating and enriching emotional tones. And he did it all by exercising a level of discipline creators with twice his experience fail to apply to themselves. They say as a writer you must be prepared to "kill your darlings." Well, Ibrahim blows up his darlings, sifts through the wreckage for the parts that still work, then sews them back together and sets them at your throat.

You'll never be happier to be in the hands of such a mad scientist.

—Phil Hester
Iowa

Phil Hester has been writing and drawing comics since the dawn of time. He has drawn Green Arrow, Swamp Thing, Ant-Man, Family Tree, *and many more, and has written titles including* Wonder Woman, The Darkness, Deathstroke, *and his co-creations* The Coffin *with artist Mike Huddleston, and* Firebreather *with artist Andy Kuhn. He was nominated for an Eisner Award for* The Wretch, *which he wrote and drew.*

THEN:
NAZI-OCCUPIED FRANCE, 1940.

98% ACCURACY PROBABILITY

83% ACCURACY PROBABILITY

46M

W:3MP

AGENT WOODARD, TARGET IN SIGHT. HE'S UP AHEAD OF YOU ON THE SOUTHWEST CORNER.

I'M IN THE BUILDING NOW, ABOUT TO REACH THE ROOF.

AND CALL ME *"AVERY,"* QUICKER ON COMMS THAN *"AGENT WOODARD."*

YOU GOT IT.

"AGENT ABDELNASSER" DOESN'T ROLL OFF THE TONGUE, EITHER.
"TARIK" WORKS.
SO THIS GUY ISAACS IS ONE OF OURS?

WAS. FORMER MOSSAD, THEN B.T.A.-DISAVOWED FOR ILLEGAL DRIFTING.

I'VE GOT A CLEAN SHOT. SHOULD I TAKE IT?

HE WAS A FRIEND. I'M NOT READY TO GIVE UP ON HIM. GONNA SEE IF I CAN TALK HIM DOWN FIRST.

73% ACCURACY PROBABILITY

83% ACCURACY PROBABILITY

68M

W:3MP

HEADS UP, WE'VE GOT INCOMING...

JESUS... THAT'S *HIM.*

IT WOULD BE SO EASY...

HEAR ME OUT: LET'S JUST LET ISAACS SHOOT HIM.

VERY FUNNY. STAY FOCUSED...

20, 32, 3, 6, 11, 4, 16, 30.

WHAT?

I'M MOVING IN.

ISAACS.
THAT YOU, AVERY?
IT'S ME, BUDDY.
TELL THE NEW GUY I SAW THE GLINT FROM HIS SCOPE.

COME BACK TO HQ WITH US AND YOU CAN TELL HIM YOURSELF.

IT ISN'T RIGHT, AVERY. THINK OF ALL OF THE LIVES WE COULD SAVE.
I KNOW HOW YOU FEEL. I *DO.* BUT *THIS* ISN'T THE WAY.

COME BACK WITH US. WE'LL FIGURE THIS OUT.
I'M SORRY, AVE...

GAHH!

SHIT.

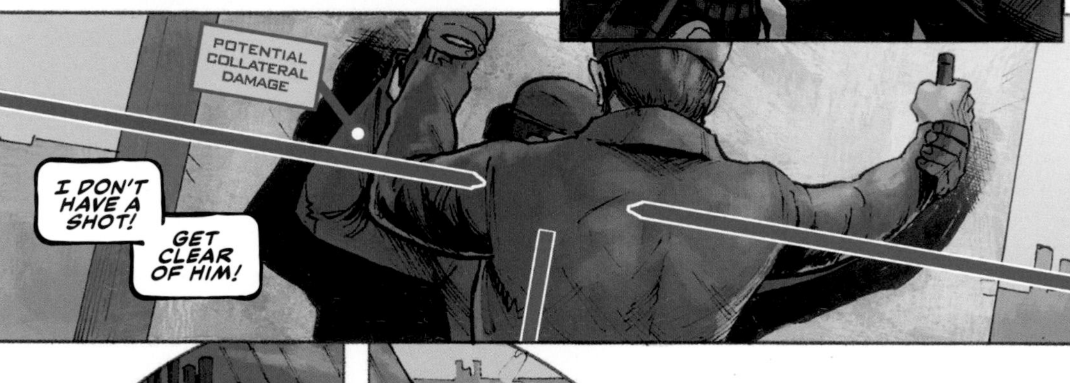

POTENTIAL COLLATERAL DAMAGE
I DON'T HAVE A SHOT!
GET CLEAR OF HIM!

SPAK
SPAK
SPAK
AVERY!

G-GO AFTER HIM.

NO, YOU COULD BLEED OUT...
IF HE...IF HE GETS CAUGHT, THE NAZIS COULD GET HIS DICHRON.

GAH!

WE HAVE TO SCRUB HIS TECH. GO.

SPAK

HUFF

DU!
HALT!
HALT!

SPAK
SPAK

AVERY!
HELP ME UP...

C'MON, LET'S GET YOU TO THE SAFE HOUSE.
HNNG! ISAACS?

I'M SORRY.
DON'T BE. FUCKER STABBED ME.

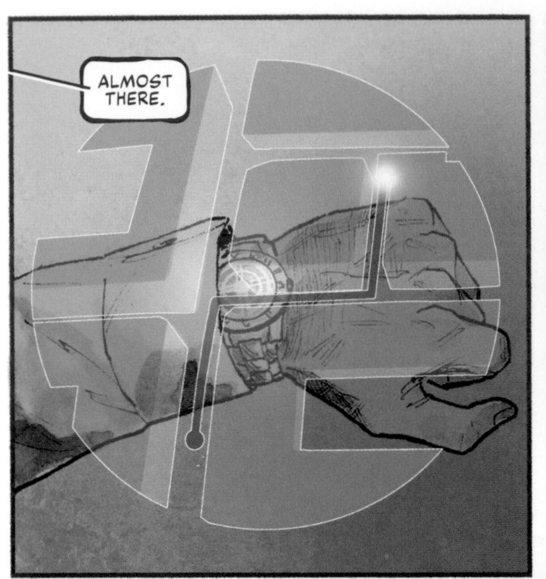
ALMOST THERE.

I'M LOSING A LOT OF BLOOD...
STAY WITH ME--WE'RE ALMOST THERE.

BEET

ALMOST THERE.
I JUST CALLED IN A CODE. MEDICAL SHOULD BE WAITING FOR US, RIGHT?
ARE YOU ABLE TO SYNC UP WITH ME?
CAN'T USE MY ARM... YOU'LL HAVE TO OVERRIDE MINE.
OVERRIDE
AVERY?
AVERY!

THEN:
BUREAU OF TEMPORAL AFFAIRS HQ.
MARYLAND, 2054.

MEDIC!

BZZ
BZZ
DEENA
Don't forget mom's appt!
SHIT.

RETRO

ACTIVE

NOW:
UPSTATE NEW YORK, 2048.
I finally tracked the plane back to its takeoff point. It's taken me weeks to get this far.
I waited in the plane for him so the accomplice who dropped him at the airfield wouldn't see me and try to intervene.
HRGK!
Shit.
AUTO PILOT

BOOOM

THEN:
MARYLAND, 2054.

"HABIBI, THIS PLACE IS *FILTHY...*"

"IT'S *NOT* FILTHY, MOM."

CONTINUITY
Memory Care Facility

WELL, THE PEOPLE ARE. LOOK AT THEM.

MOM, *KHALAS.*

THIS IS THE COMMON AREA, AS YOU CAN SEE. WE HAVE MOVIE NIGHTS, BINGO, LIVE MUSIC...

MOM, BABA'S **GONE.** REMEMBER? HE WAS IN A CAR ACCIDENT...
...

OF COURSE I **REMEMBER!** AND YOU WANT ME TO LEAVE THE HOUSE WE SHARED TOGETHER!
YOUR SISTER WOULD **NEVER** DO THIS TO ME, **WALLAH.**

MOM, **DEENA** IS THE ONE WHO **FOUND** THIS PLACE.
SHE **TOLD** YOU THAT.

PLEASE, I WANT TO GO HOME NOW. TAKE ME HOME.
BZZ
BZZ

WORK
Avery is out of surgery, awake.
OKAY, OKAY. LET'S GO...

"KNOCK KNOCK."

PERMISSION TO COME ABOARD?

AYYY, THERE HE IS.

HOW'RE YOU FEELING?

HEH. LIKE I WAS ***STABBED.***

THANKS FOR SAVING MY ASS BACK THERE.

I SHOULD BE THANKING ***YOU***--GETTING YOU OUT OF THERE WAS THE ONLY PART OF THAT MISSION THAT DIDN'T FEEL WRONG.

A BIG PART OF ME WANTED TO LET ISAACS GO THROUGH WITH IT.

HEY, ME TOO. BUT IF WE HAD, THEY'D JUST SEND SOMEONE ELSE BACK TO UNDO IT.

YEAH. IT'S JUST... ***KNOWING*** WE HAVE THE POWER TO CHANGE THINGS BUT NOT HAVING THE CHOICE...

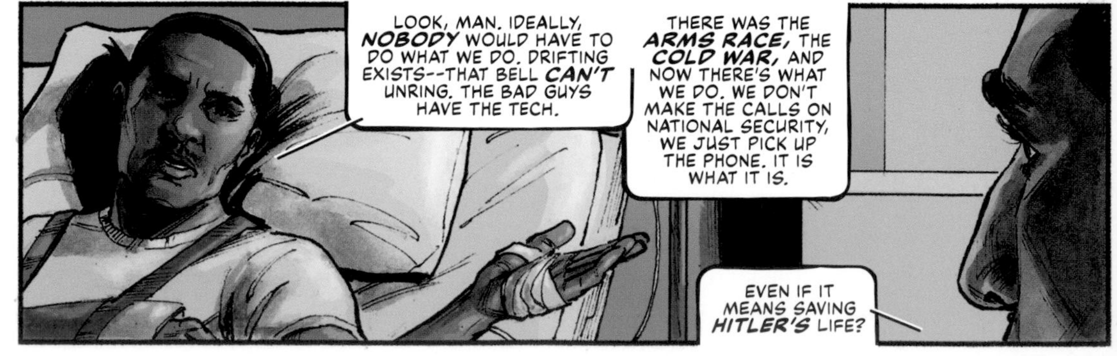

UNFORTUNATELY, YEAH. YOU'VE GOT TO HOLD ON TO THE WINS, 'RIK.
YOU REMEMBER WHEN THOSE HILLBILLIES HIT THE TWO NUCLEAR REACTORS IN THE NORTHEAST IN '48?

BEFORE MY TIME, BUT I READ ABOUT IT.
THE BTA SAVED HUNDREDS OF LIVES BY GOING BACK TO STOP THAT FROM HAPPENING. THOUSANDS IF YOU COUNT THE FALLOUT THAT WOULD'VE COME AFTER.
YOU'RE RIGHT. I BELIEVE IN WHAT WE DO, MAN. I DO. I JUST...SOMETIMES I WONDER WHAT KEEPS US FROM BECOMING ISAACS, Y'KNOW?
DRIFTING, THE WHIPLASH... IT'S DISORIENTING. IT MAKES ME THINK: DID IT PUSH HIM TO BREAK? WILL IT PUSH US?
REACH INTO THE BREAST POCKET THERE...

20, 32, 6, 3, 16, 4, 11, 30.

20, 32, 6, 3, 16, 4, 11, 30
YEAH?

WHEN I FEEL LIKE I'M SLIPPING, I CHECK MY MEMORY AGAINST THAT. IT HELPS WITH SEQUENCING WHEN THINGS GET FUZZY FROM ALL THE DRIFTING. YOU KEEP THAT--I'VE GOT COPIES.
AND WHEN YOU CAN'T REMEMBER THE SEQUENCE ANYMORE, IT'S PROBABLY TIME TO GET OUT.
I'LL TRY IT. THANKS.

I SLIPPED UP TODAY, ISAACS CUTTING ME LIKE THAT.
I MIXED UP THE NUMBERS. AND NOW I'M SITTING IN A HOSPITAL BED. THINK IT'S TIME I LEAVE THE FIELD FOR A DESK. NOBODY SHOULD DO THIS JOB FOR TOO LONG...

"...IT CAN START MESSING WITH YOUR HEAD."
NOW: MANHATTAN, 2048.
Back where they dropped me off.
Back at the beginning. Again.
Withdrawals from my post-drift meds. Or maybe the whiplash from being shot in the head what feels like only a minute ago.
REEEE
OOOH
ROUGH NIGHT?
NYPD
Dichron still not working. Just like he said it wouldn't.
20, 32, 6, 3, 16, 4, 11, 30.
So far, so good.

My practiced routine.
ORDER NUMBER 32!
Food.
WATCH IT, ASSHOLE!
EXCUSE ME, SORRY.
YEAH, SOME ASSHOLE JUST WALKED RIGHT INTO ME...
Money.
Please Wait To Be Seated
Coat Check
VALE
Transportation.

Hiding inside the plane turned out to be a poor plan last time.
I need to work back farther. Get him in the airfield parking lot.
I tried alerting the authorities and saving myself the trouble, but an Arab man with no I.D. calling in a terrorist attack went about as well as one might expect.
SOVEREIGNTY IS NOT GIVEN. IT IS TAKEN
Thankfully, I woke up in the alley again.
I can't get a gun without I.D., so a knife from a pawn shop is the best I can do.

GAAAHHH!
I'm hoping that a blade to the trapezius makes him unable to draw the gun I know he has under his left shoulder.
There it is.
BLAM

Not enough time before the next attack to dispose of anything properly.
The bomb wasn't armed yet, so I drop it in the sewer and hope that's enough.

The second attack happens in thirteen minutes...

...I'm twenty-two minutes away.

SHIT.

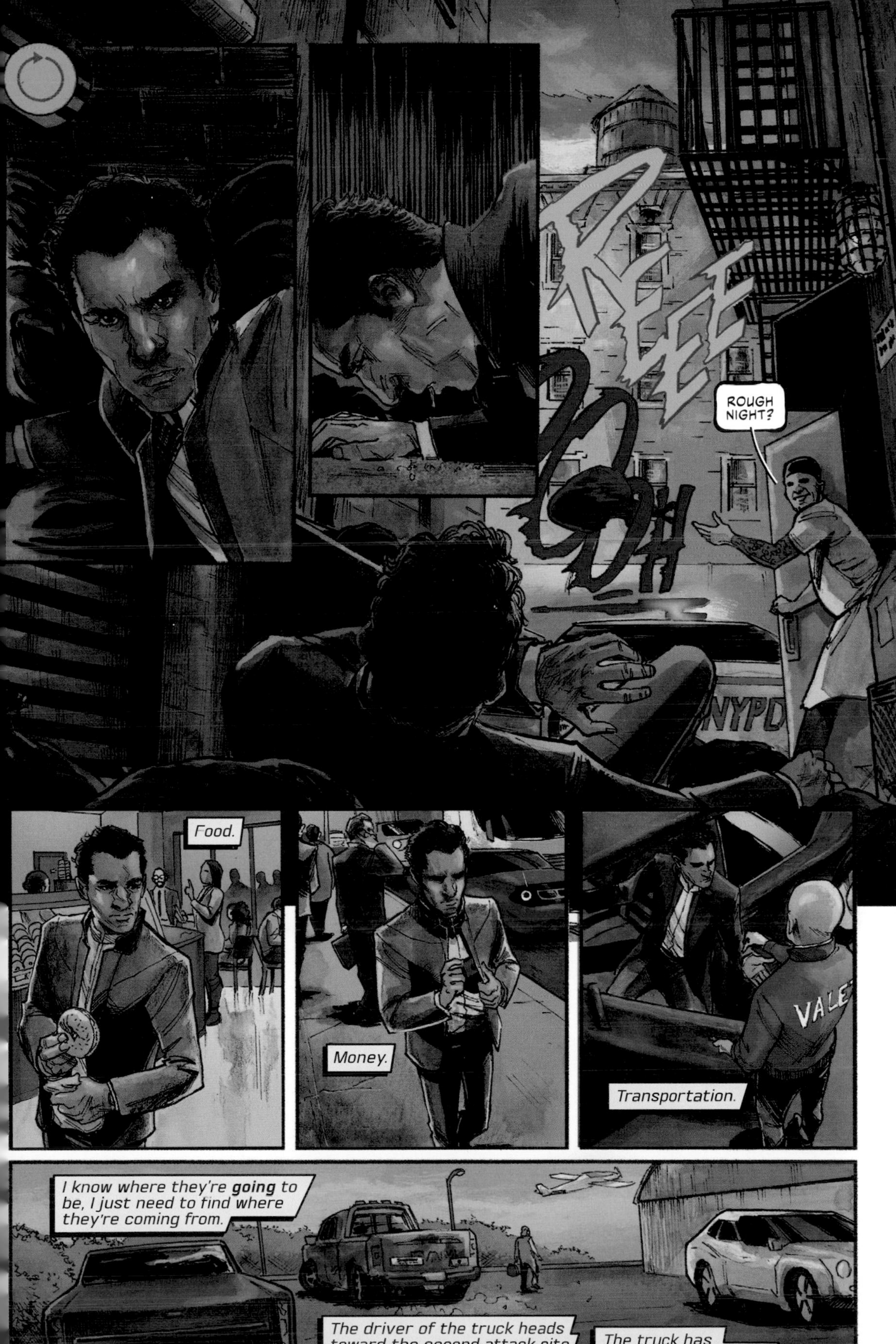
REEE
OOH
ROUGH NIGHT?
NYPD
Food.
Money.
VALE
Transportation.
I know where they're **going** to be, I just need to find where they're coming from.
The driver of the truck heads toward the second attack site after dropping off the pilot.
The truck has Pennsylvania plates, and it approaches from the east.

I start as early as I can and head toward the most likely route the truck would've taken to get to the airfield.
With no BTA resources at my disposal, I have to find the attackers the old fashioned way: look.

I divide the area into quadrants and search until the moment of the second attack...
...then the day resets, and I have to start over again.

No luck.

Still nothing.

Bingo.

I know these guys are heavily armed.
DON'T TREAD ON ME
I have to assume they have ground sensors. Given the extent and nature of their attacks, possibly tripwires and other traps.
Time to do some recon.

THEN:
MARYLAND, 2057.
5:59 AM

6:00 AM

0600
SNOOZE

NEW VOICEMAIL:
DEENA

"MOM FELL AGAIN IN THE MIDDLE OF THE NIGHT. THEY **TRIED** CALLING YOU...YOU **NEED** TO GET OVER THERE ASAP. AND **CALL ME BACK.**"

SHIT.

DEENA, I **CALLED** THEM BACK.
MOM IS **FINE.** IT'S A NICE FACILITY-- THEY HAVE A GOOD NURSING STAFF THERE.
YOU STILL NEED TO GO AND CHECK ON HER.

I'VE GOT AN IMPORTANT WORK THING, THEN I'LL GO SEE HER, OKAY?
Y'KNOW, FOR SOMEONE WHOSE JOB IS "RISK ASSESSMENT AND TIME MANAGEMENT," YOU'RE PRETTY SHITTY AT MANAGING YOUR TIME TO GO ASSESS MOM.
DEENA, YOU HAVE **NO IDEA** WHAT MY JOB IS LIKE, OKAY?

HOW COULD I WHEN YOU WON'T TALK ABOUT IT?
I CAN'T. IT'S CLASSIFIED, YOU KNOW THAT.
ANYWAY. WHETHER I GET THERE BEFORE OR AFTER MY MEETING, IT'S NOT GOING TO MAKE MOM UN-FALL. SHE BARELY RECOGNIZES ME ANYMORE ANYWAY. AND YOU KNOW WHAT?

AT LEAST I'M HERE. YOU'RE WELCOME TO MOVE BACK ANY TIME TO DO THINGS YOUR WAY.

THAT IS NOT FAIR. GOD, YOU'RE SUCH A DICK. JUST GET OVER THERE.
KLIK

SIGH

AGENT OLMOS?

HI, TARIK ABDELNASSER.

LUCIA. NICE TO MEET YOU.

WANNA TAKE A CLOSER LOOK?
CAN WE? I'M STILL WAITING ON MY SECURITY CLEARANCE TO GO THROUGH.

NO WORRIES-- WE CAN BOTH ENTER ON MINE.

WOW...
...SO THIS IS HOW THE MAGIC HAPPENS.
YEP. WE CALL IT "HIGGY" AFTER--

PETER HIGGS. "ONE OF FIVE TEMPORAL ACCELERATORS IN THE WORLD, THE OTHERS BELONGING TO THE TEMPORAL AGENCIES OF THE UK, JAPAN, CHINA, AND THE FORMER SOVIET REPUBLIC OF RUSSIA, RESPECTIVELY."

I READ THE TRAINING MATERIALS.

GREAT.
LET'S HEAD FOR THE CHAMBERS AND WE'LL TAKE YOU ON YOUR FIRST DRIFT SO YOU CAN FIND YOUR SEA LEGS.

HAVE YOU FINISHED THE FULL COURSE OF YOUR PRE-DRIFT MEDS?
ALL THIRTY DAYS' WORTH. BEEN PISSING BLUE FOR WEEKS.
HA. YEAH, THAT'LL WEAR OFF. ANY QUESTIONS ABOUT ANYTHING?
OH, I'VE GOT PLENTY.

I KNOW DRIFTING IS ONLY POSSIBLE TO SINGULAR POINTS IN THE PAST, AND THEN BACK TO THE PRESENT. NO HOPPING THROUGH HISTORY...
...BUT I DIDN'T FIND ANYTHING IN THE READING ABOUT PEOPLE DRIFTING HERE ***FROM*** THE FUTURE.

SO, THE BTA MONITORS ALL SIGNALS FROM THE OTHER AGENCIES THAT CONNECT BACK TO THEIR RESPECTIVE UNIQUE TEMPORAL ACCELERATOR SIGNATURES...
RIGHT.

THUS FAR, ALL DRIFTING PICKED UP BY OUR ANALYSTS IS CONSISTENT WITH THOSE SIGNATURES--NOTHING INDICATES DRIFTS FROM OUR FUTURE.
BUT, THE BTA HAS BEEN MONITORING SOME TEMPORAL ***ANOMALIES*** RECENTLY--PEBBLES DROPPED INTO THE TIME STREAM, ESSENTIALLY.

ARE THESE PEBBLES MAKING RIPPLES?
THAT'S THE CONCERN. WE DON'T KNOW WHO OR ***WHAT*** IS CAUSING THEM. COULD BE NEW TECH FROM MOSCOW OR BEIJING. BUT THE THEORY IS SOMEONE'S COMING ***BACK*** TO OUR ***PRESENT.***
EVERY TIME WE GET CLOSE, THE PEBBLES DISAPPEAR.

YOU READY TO TIME TRAVEL?

ONCE WE'RE INSIDE, I'LL ENTER THE DRIFT COORDINATES INTO MY DICHRON, AND YOURS WILL PROMPT YOU TO ACCEPT THE DRIFT.
WHERE ARE WE HEADED?
PHILLY. FIFTEEN YEARS AGO.
ANYTHING SPECIAL ABOUT IT?
JUST AN ORDINARY DAY.
HIT CONFIRM AND SLIDE IT TO THE RIGHT.
NOW HANG ON TO SOME-THING.

THEN:
BTA DRIFT SITE. PHILADELPHIA, 2042.

FIRST DRIFT'S ALWAYS JARRING, BUT PRETTY SOON YOU WON'T EVEN FEEL IT.
YOU OKAY?
DRIFT SITES CAN REQUIRE LOTS OF CAUTION WHEN COMING AND GOING.
BUT THE BTA OWNS THIS BUILDING, SO WE CAN BE PRETTY CASUAL IN HERE.
YOU WERE RECRUITED FROM THE C.I.A. TOO, RIGHT?
YEAH, COUNTER-TERRORISM.
HOW WAS THE TRANSITION FOR YOU?
HEH. RIGHT.
WELL, WITH THE EXCEPTION OF MOVING THROUGH TIME--
MUCH OF THE SKILL SET IS THE SAME. WE WORK TO MAINTAIN NATIONAL SECURITY, RUN OPS AGAINST HOSTILE NATIONS, AVERT CATASTROPHES...
...WE SAVE LIVES.

SOMETHING THAT NO OTHER AGENCY CAN PREPARE YOU FOR ARE SOME OF THE DECISIONS YOU'LL HAVE TO MAKE.
YOU'LL HAVE TO PREVENT THE DEATHS OF TERRIBLE PEOPLE, KNOWING WHAT THEY'LL GO ON TO DO IF YOU LET THEM LIVE. THERE ARE THINGS YOU'LL WANT TO GO BACK AND CHANGE. PEOPLE YOU'LL WANT TO SAVE...

...BUT WE CAN NEVER USE THIS FOR PERSONAL REASONS. YOU JUST HAVE TO REMEMBER--WHAT WE DO IS IMPORTANT. YOU WON'T ALWAYS LIKE IT OR AGREE WITH IT, BUT IT'S ALL FOR THE GREATER GOOD.

BZZ
BZZ
NEW ORDERS?

THEY NEED US BACK AT HQ FOR A BRIEFING WITH THE SPECIAL AGENT IN CHARGE.
MIND IF I DO THE HONORS THIS TIME?
BY ALL MEANS.

RIGHT BEHIND YOU.

THEN:
BTA HQ.
2057.
DOING ALL RIGHT?
FIRST ONE'S ALWAYS THE HARDEST. DON'T FORGET YOUR POST-DRIFT MEDS. THEY'LL HELP YOU RECALIBRATE.
BETTER, THANKS.
GOT IT.
CHIEF.
BUREAU OF TEMPORAL AFFAIRS
'RIK. AGENT OLMOS.
RICK?

KIM'S TEAM PICKED UP MORE OF THE ANOMALIES WE'VE BEEN TRACING. I'LL LET HER FILL YOU IN. KIM?

RIGHT.

SO, WE'VE BEEN MONITORING FOR THESE UNIQUE SIGNATURES POPPING UP IN THE TIME STREAM.

THE BLUE WIDGETS ARE OUR AGENTS IN THE FIELD, AND OUR ALLIES, IN VARIOUS POINTS IN TIME.

EACH HAS A SIGNATURE SPECIFIC TO ITS RESPECTIVE TEMPORAL ACCELERATOR-- LONDON, TOKYO, OR IN OUR CASE, HIGGY.

THESE ***RED*** WIDGETS ARE THE ANOMALIES. NOTICE HOW THEY DON'T HAVE ACCELERATOR SIGNATURES?

PEBBLES IN THE STREAM.

EXACTLY. WITH NO TRACEABLE TETHER TO ANY OF THE OTHER ACCELERATORS, WE DON'T KNOW WHO OR WHAT THESE ANOMALIES ARE.

THE DIRECTOR HAS BEEN IN TOUCH WITH HER COUNTERPARTS AT MI-9 AND JAPAN'S JIKAN INTELLIGENCE. THEY SAY IT'S NOT THEIR PEOPLE AND ARE ASKING US TO KEEP THEM UPDATED.

THAT LEAVES BEIJING AND MOSCOW.

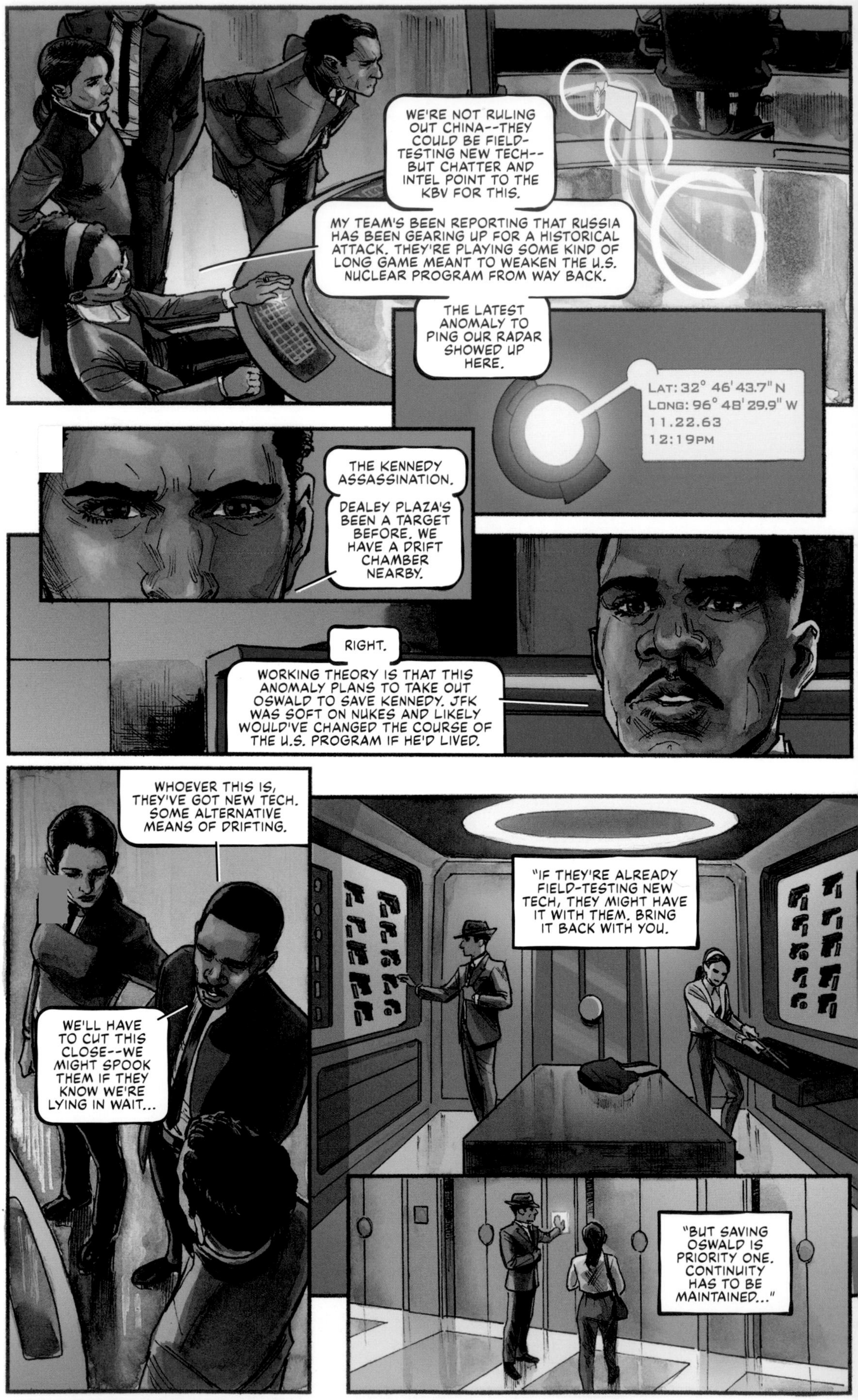

WE'RE NOT RULING OUT CHINA--THEY COULD BE FIELD-TESTING NEW TECH--BUT CHATTER AND INTEL POINT TO THE KBV FOR THIS.

MY TEAM'S BEEN REPORTING THAT RUSSIA HAS BEEN GEARING UP FOR A HISTORICAL ATTACK. THEY'RE PLAYING SOME KIND OF LONG GAME MEANT TO WEAKEN THE U.S. NUCLEAR PROGRAM FROM WAY BACK.

THE LATEST ANOMALY TO PING OUR RADAR SHOWED UP HERE.

LAT: 32° 46' 43.7" N
LONG: 96° 48' 29.9" W
11.22.63
12:19PM

THE KENNEDY ASSASSINATION.

DEALEY PLAZA'S BEEN A TARGET BEFORE. WE HAVE A DRIFT CHAMBER NEARBY.

RIGHT.

WORKING THEORY IS THAT THIS ANOMALY PLANS TO TAKE OUT OSWALD TO SAVE KENNEDY. JFK WAS SOFT ON NUKES AND LIKELY WOULD'VE CHANGED THE COURSE OF THE U.S. PROGRAM IF HE'D LIVED.

WHOEVER THIS IS, THEY'VE GOT NEW TECH. SOME ALTERNATIVE MEANS OF DRIFTING.

WE'LL HAVE TO CUT THIS CLOSE--WE MIGHT SPOOK THEM IF THEY KNOW WE'RE LYING IN WAIT...

"IF THEY'RE ALREADY FIELD-TESTING NEW TECH, THEY MIGHT HAVE IT WITH THEM. BRING IT BACK WITH YOU.

"BUT SAVING OSWALD IS PRIORITY ONE. CONTINUITY HAS TO BE MAINTAINED..."

THEN: DALLAS, 1963.

"...KENNEDY HAS TO DIE IN THAT PLAZA."

HERTZ

KEEP TO FIRST NAMES ON COMMS-- EASIER THAT WAY.

GOT IT.

OUR BEST BET IS GONNA BE TO GO FOR OSWALD DIRECTLY. I'LL ENTER THE BOOK DEPOSITORY, YOU COVER THE REAR EXIT.

TRY TO MAINTAIN A LINE OF SIGHT TO THE MOTORCADE IF YOU CAN.

PROTOCOL SAYS WE SWEEP THE BUILDING *TOGETHER.*

WE DON'T HAVE THE TIME. I'LL HEAD STRAIGHT FOR THE 6TH FLOOR...

...CHECK IN ON COMMS WHEN YOU REACH YOUR POSITION!

OSWALD IS INCAPACITATED. NO SIGN OF--

CREEEAK

HRKKK!
AMERICAN HISTORY
TARIK?
TARIK?!
THWAKK
AMERICAN HISTORY
HNGG!
AMERICAN HISTORY

GYAH!

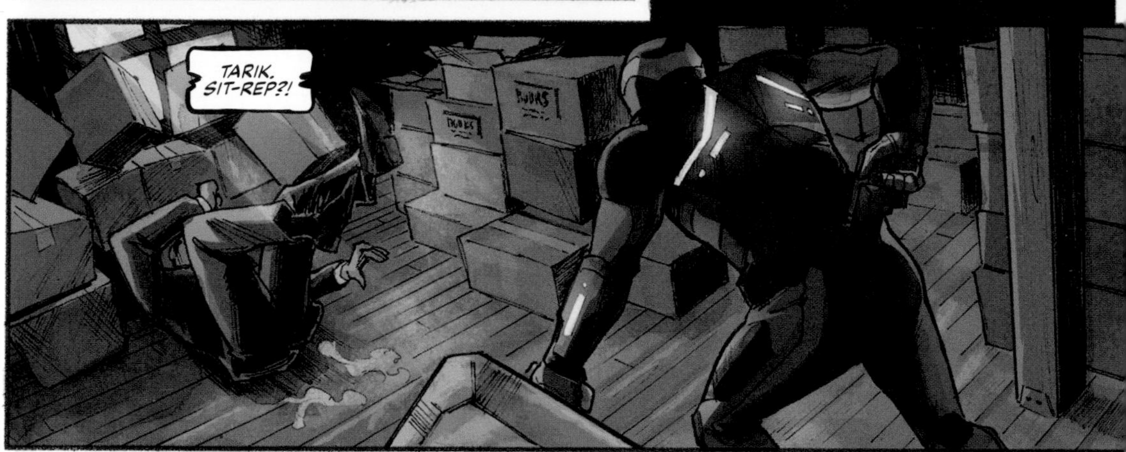
TARIK. SIT-REP?!

REPEAT: SITUATION REPORT!
12:26:32
TARIK!

HNGGG--THE ANOMALY IS ON THE MOVE. OSWALD IS OUT COLD AND THE MOTORCADE IS APPROACHING--I HAVE TO TAKE THE SHOT.

DO YOU HAVE A SHOT?

POOR COVER. FINDING A BETTER POSITION.

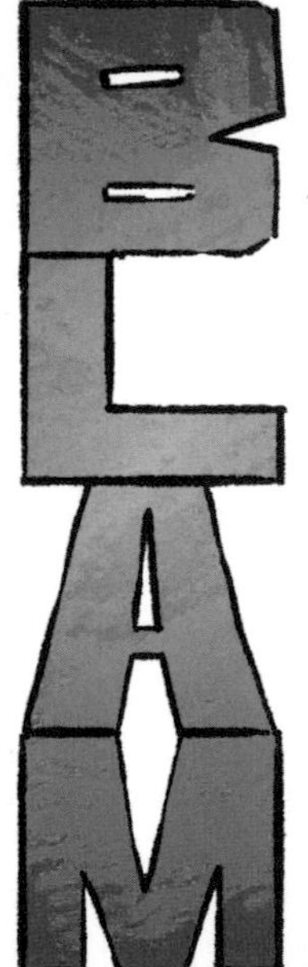
BLAM

BLAM

JESUS...

...THAT'S HIM.

KLAK
WHAM

THREE O'CLOCK!

HNNNGG!

KLAK

TARIK!

I'LL MEET YOU BACK AT THE DRIFT SITE!

TARIK, **TELL ME WHERE YOU ARE.** I CAN GET TO YOU.

HOOONK

HONK
HOOO ONK
808
808
KRASH

TARIK, DO YOU COPY?!
HEADING BACK TO YOU.

WHAT THE HELL WAS *THAT?!*

I DON'T KNOW. HE HAD SOME KIND OF SUIT ON, IT--
DEET
NOT THE ANOMALY, I'M TALKING ABOUT YOU.
FIRST YOU BREAK PROCEDURE ON THE BUILDING SWEEP--I GET THAT--BUT THEN YOU RUN OFF, INJURED, TO CHASE AN UNSUB USING UNKNOWN TECH, WITH NO COMMUNICATION WHATSOEVER.
LOOK, I ADAPTED TO THE SITUATION. YOU KNOW THAT'S PART OF THE JOB.
NOT LIKE THAT. THE TWO OF US COULD HAVE COORDINATED. TOGETHER WE MIGHT'VE CORNERED HIM. BUT YOU WENT LONE WOLF AND LEFT ME IN THE DARK.
THAT WAS A SHIT SHOW, TARIK.
IT WOULDN'T HAVE MATTERED. HE DISAPPEARED.
THAT'S WHAT I'M SAYING. YOU LOST HIM. TOGETHER WE--
NO, LUCIA-- HE LITERALLY VANISHED INTO THIN AIR.
WHAT?

THEN:
BTA HQ, 2057.
THE SUIT HE WAS WEARING...IT MUST BE SOME KIND OF ADVANCED TECH.
AND HE LEFT ONE BEHIND.
HERE. YOU TAKE IT IN.
IS THIS SUPPOSED TO BE MY CONSOLATION PRIZE?
PEACE OFFERING?
LOOK. I WANT TO BE EFFECTIVE HERE. AND I WANT TO LEARN. I CAN'T DO EITHER IF YOU'RE GOING TO BE A ONE-MAN SHOW.
I'M GOING TO BE HONEST IN MY MISSION REPORT.
I WOULD EXPECT NOTHING LESS.
TAKE THE CASE DOWN TO THE LAB AND THEN DEBRIEF WITH AVERY. I'VE GOTTA LEAVE FOR A BIT, BUT I'LL BE BACK BY THE TIME THE LAB'S HAD A CHANCE TO ANALYZE IT...

LOOKS LIKE IT WASN'T TOO BAD. ARE YOU FEELING OKAY?

HEH, OKAY. THANKS?

OH, ***HABIBI.*** YOUR FACE IS BETTER.

I'M GONNA USE YOUR BATHROOM, OKAY?

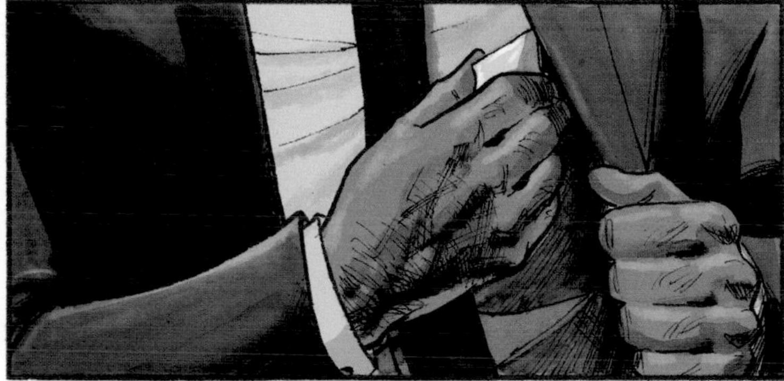

20, 32, 6, 3,
16, 4, 11, 30
SIGH
MOM, DID THEY LEAVE THE FIRST AID SUPPLIES OUT?
TEN GRAND A MONTH FOR THIS PLACE, YOU'D THINK THEY'D CLEAN UP AFTER THEMSELVES.

WHA--?
BZZ BZZ
Incoming Call
AVERY
CHIEF.
'RIK. WE NEED YOU BACK AT HQ. LAB'S READY FOR US.
COME BY MY OFFICE FIRST.
YOU GOT IT. ON MY WAY.
I HAVE TO GO BACK TO WORK NOW. DO YOU NEED ANYTHING BEFORE I LEAVE?
I STILL CLOSE THE SIDE.
OKAY, MOM. UHIBBUKA.

NOW: RURAL PENNSYLVANIA, 2048.
This place is heavily fortified. I have to be extremely careful.

I've managed to identify what I think are a few blind spots on their surveillance system.
Luckily, a side effect of their particular ideology is a resistance to modern tech.
They prefer analog.

Which means their old hard-wired cameras are a little easier to slip.
KLIK
Landmines.
SHIT.
BOOM

Ground sensors.

Missed camera.

Man unaccounted for.
MOTHER FUCKER!

This time they decide to interrogate me.
WHO THE FUCK ARE YOU?!

I take this as an opportunity to get some answers for myself.
YOU'RE ON SOVEREIGN LAND, YOU FUCKIN' CAMEL JOCKEY. WE DON'T ANSWER TO OR ACKNOWLEDGE THE "LAWS" OF THE U.S. GOVERNMENT.

I learn that they're radical doomsday preppers. Their attacks are meant to cause reactor meltdowns at major power hubs...

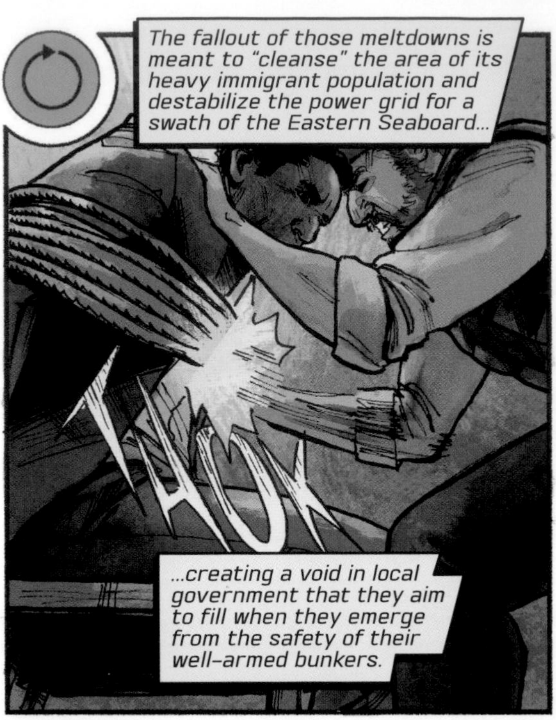
The fallout of those meltdowns is meant to "cleanse" the area of its heavy immigrant population and destabilize the power grid for a swath of the Eastern Seaboard...
THOCK
...creating a void in local government that they aim to fill when they emerge from the safety of their well-armed bunkers.

KRAK
There's a whole network of them. These two are just the first of many coordinated attacks in an effort to build a pure, free America.
An America that "resembles that of our founding fathers." Without "foreigners" like me.

THUMP
TELL ME WHO THE FUCK YOU ARE!
Then I see it.

Their munitions cache.
Guns, magnetic disc-grenades, other projectiles and explosives.

I've got all of the pieces now: Five men in total, their plan, and their stockpile.
Only had to get the shit kicked out of me to do it.
I'M A TIME-TRAVELER FROM THE FUTURE HERE TO STOP YOU.
LAUGH IT UP, MOTHERFUCKER.

BLAM

REEE
WOOH
ROUGH NIGHT?
How many is this? How many times have I died?
20, 32, 6, 3, 16, 4, 11, 30.
Am I losing it?
Is it the looping? All of my previous drifting catching up with me? Is mom's dementia hereditary?
Am I becoming **him?**
Maybe it's all of it.

It doesn't matter right now.
It doesn't change what I have to do...

Complete the circuit before the anomalies come back for me.
FIVE, FOUR, THREE, TWO...

FIVE, FOUR, THREE, TWO...
EARL?! **HELL** WAS THAT?!

I have to break the loop.

SPAK

I know where they're going to be, how many they are, which cameras to dodge.
The landmines. The sensors. All of it.

Timed it all out.

I've run it through.
FIVE, FOUR, THREE, TWO...

BLAM

BLAM BLAM
That leaves one more. Somewhere upstairs.

Shit.
This is new.

I didn't account for **this**.

SADIE!

HEY!

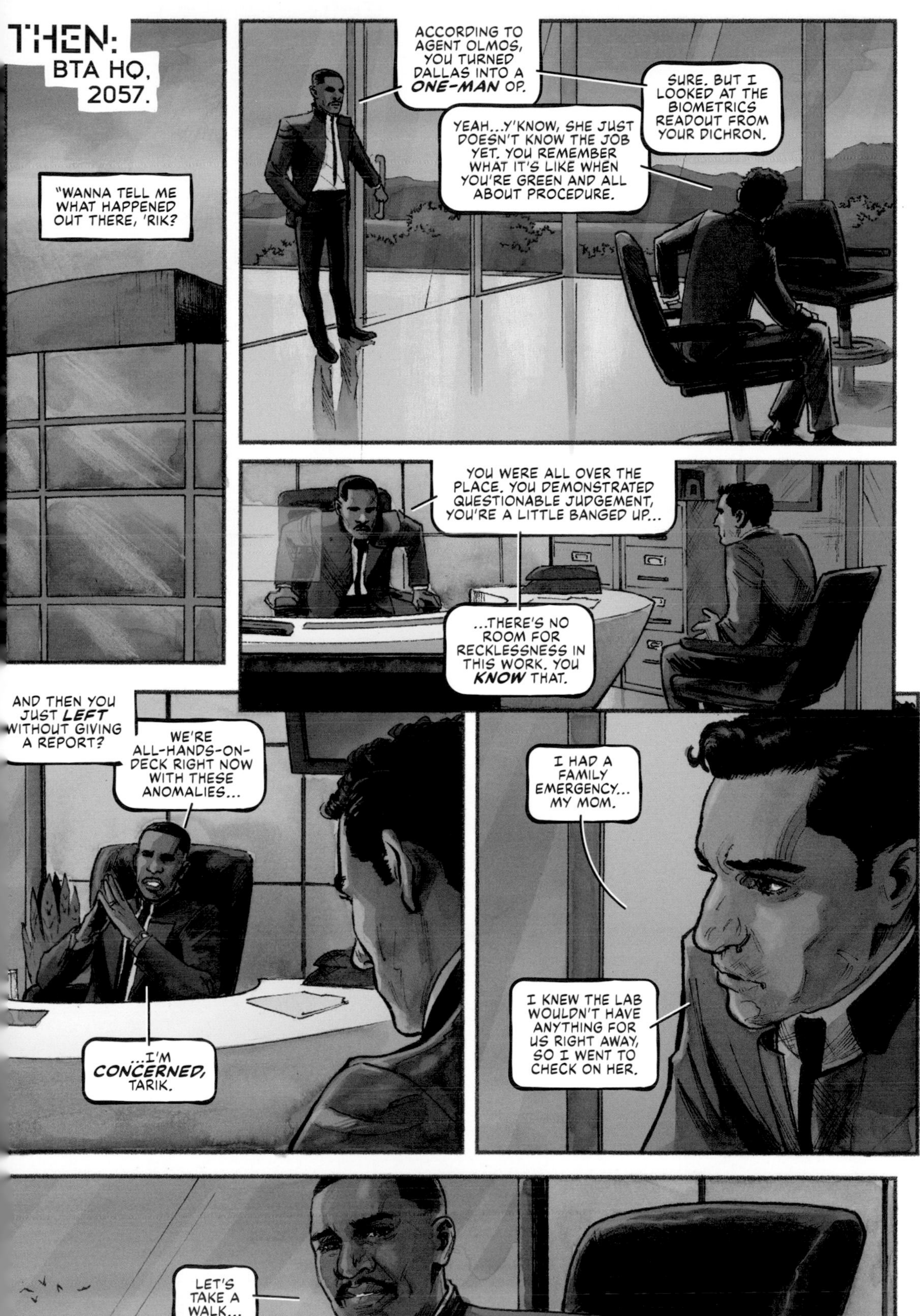
THEN: BTA HQ, 2057.
"WANNA TELL ME WHAT HAPPENED OUT THERE, 'RIK?
ACCORDING TO AGENT OLMOS, YOU TURNED DALLAS INTO A ONE-MAN OP.
YEAH...Y'KNOW, SHE JUST DOESN'T KNOW THE JOB YET. YOU REMEMBER WHAT IT'S LIKE WHEN YOU'RE GREEN AND ALL ABOUT PROCEDURE.
SURE. BUT I LOOKED AT THE BIOMETRICS READOUT FROM YOUR DICHRON.
YOU WERE ALL OVER THE PLACE. YOU DEMONSTRATED QUESTIONABLE JUDGEMENT, YOU'RE A LITTLE BANGED UP...
...THERE'S NO ROOM FOR RECKLESSNESS IN THIS WORK. YOU KNOW THAT.
AND THEN YOU JUST LEFT WITHOUT GIVING A REPORT?
WE'RE ALL-HANDS-ON-DECK RIGHT NOW WITH THESE ANOMALIES...
...I'M CONCERNED, TARIK.
I HAD A FAMILY EMERGENCY... MY MOM.
I KNEW THE LAB WOULDN'T HAVE ANYTHING FOR US RIGHT AWAY, SO I WENT TO CHECK ON HER.
LET'S TAKE A WALK...

ALRIGHT, WORK STAYS IN THE OFFICE. FRIEND TO FRIEND, WHAT'S GOING ON WITH YOU?
YOU OKAY?
YEAH...I JUST-- MY MOM HAS DEMENTIA.
SHE'S HAD IT FOR A WHILE, AND I'VE GOT HER IN A GOOD FACILITY, BUT... I DON'T KNOW. MAYBE IT'S DISTRACTING ME.
MAYBE THE JOB, DRIFTING...MIGHT BE THAT IT'S STARTING TO GET TO ME A LITTLE.
YOU STILL USING THE SEQUENCING TRICK I SHOWED YOU?
YEAH, EVERY TIME. SO FAR, SO GOOD.
LIKE I TOLD YOU WHEN I GAVE YOU THAT CARD: NOBODY'S MEANT TO DO THIS JOB FOR TOO LONG...
...YOU EVER THINK ABOUT GETTING OUT OF THE FIELD? I CAN PUT IN A GOOD WORD FOR YOU.
I'M NOT COMMAND MATERIAL, AND I DON'T THINK I COULD RIDE A DESK.
NO OFFENSE.
HEH. NONE TAKEN.

I DIDN'T THINK I COULD, EITHER, BUT I ALSO LIKE KNOWING WHAT DAY IT IS.
YOU SHOULD THINK ABOUT IT.
EITHER WAY, I CAN'T TAKE THE PAY CUT...MY MOM'S CARE FACILITY IS ASTRONOMICALLY EXPENSIVE.
YOU GETTING ANY HELP FROM YOUR SISTER?
PSHH. SHE'S SPLITTING THE COST WITH ME, BUT SHE'S NOT HERE.
SHE'S GOT A GOOD JOB IN LONDON, SO MOSTLY SHE JUST GUILT-TRIPS ME FROM OVERSEAS ABOUT HOW I'M NOT DOING ENOUGH.
I HEAR YOU. THAT'S A TOUGH SPOT. LET ME KNOW HOW I CAN HELP.
MEANTIME, THE LAB'S READY FOR US...

DOC. WHAT HAVE YOU GOT FOR US?
CHIEF. AGENT ABDELNASSER.
DR. MIRWANI.
AGENT OLMOS HERE BROUGHT IN QUITE A PIECE OF TECH.
I'VE NEVER SEEN ANYTHING LIKE THIS. THE SAME ANTIMICROBIAL ALLOY THAT OUR DRIFT CHAMBERS ARE MADE OF APPEARS TO BE WOVEN THROUGHOUT THIS SUIT.
THERE ARE COMPARTMENTS FOR WEAPONS AND OTHER PORTABLE ITEMS.
AND IF YOU TOUCH THERE ON THE FOREARM...
...IT HAS WHAT IS OSTENSIBLY A MORE ADVANCED DICHRON BUILT INTO IT.
THIS SUIT IS EFFECTIVELY A WEARABLE DRIFT CHAMBER. NO CLUNKY BOX TO STEP IN AND OUT OF, NO HIDDEN DRIFT SITES...
...THEORETICALLY, IT CAN GO ANYWHERE.

THE ANOMALY WE CHASED WAS WEARING ONE VERY SIMILAR TO THIS, BUT IT WAS COLORED A BIT DIFFERENTLY, AND IT HAD A KIND OF HELMET.

AH...

...LIKE THIS?

HEH. YEP.

WHAT CAN YOU TELL US ABOUT ITS ORIGIN?

THIS THING IS SO ADVANCED, I COULDN'T TELL YOU WHERE IT'S FROM, LET ALONE ***WHEN*** IT'S FROM.

IF I WERE TO DISMANTLE IT, I MIGHT BE ABLE TO GLEAN ***SOME*** INFORMATION ON WHERE THE PIECES ORIGINATED...PART NUMBERS, MANUFACTURER STAMPS, THAT SORT OF THING.

BUT I ***DO*** FEEL CONFIDENT IN ASSERTING THAT THIS WAS ***NOT*** THE WORK OF THE KBV.

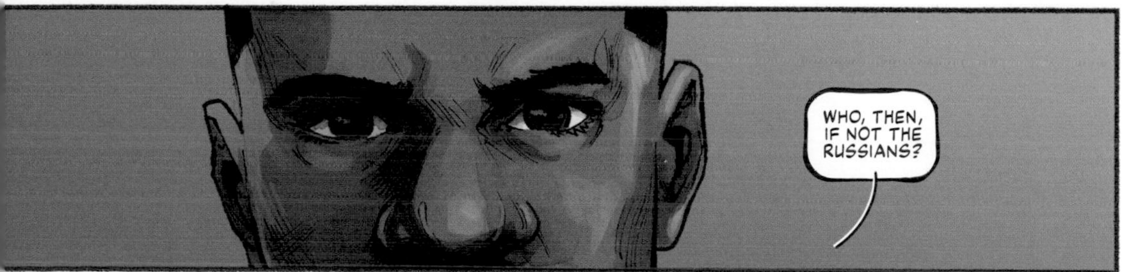

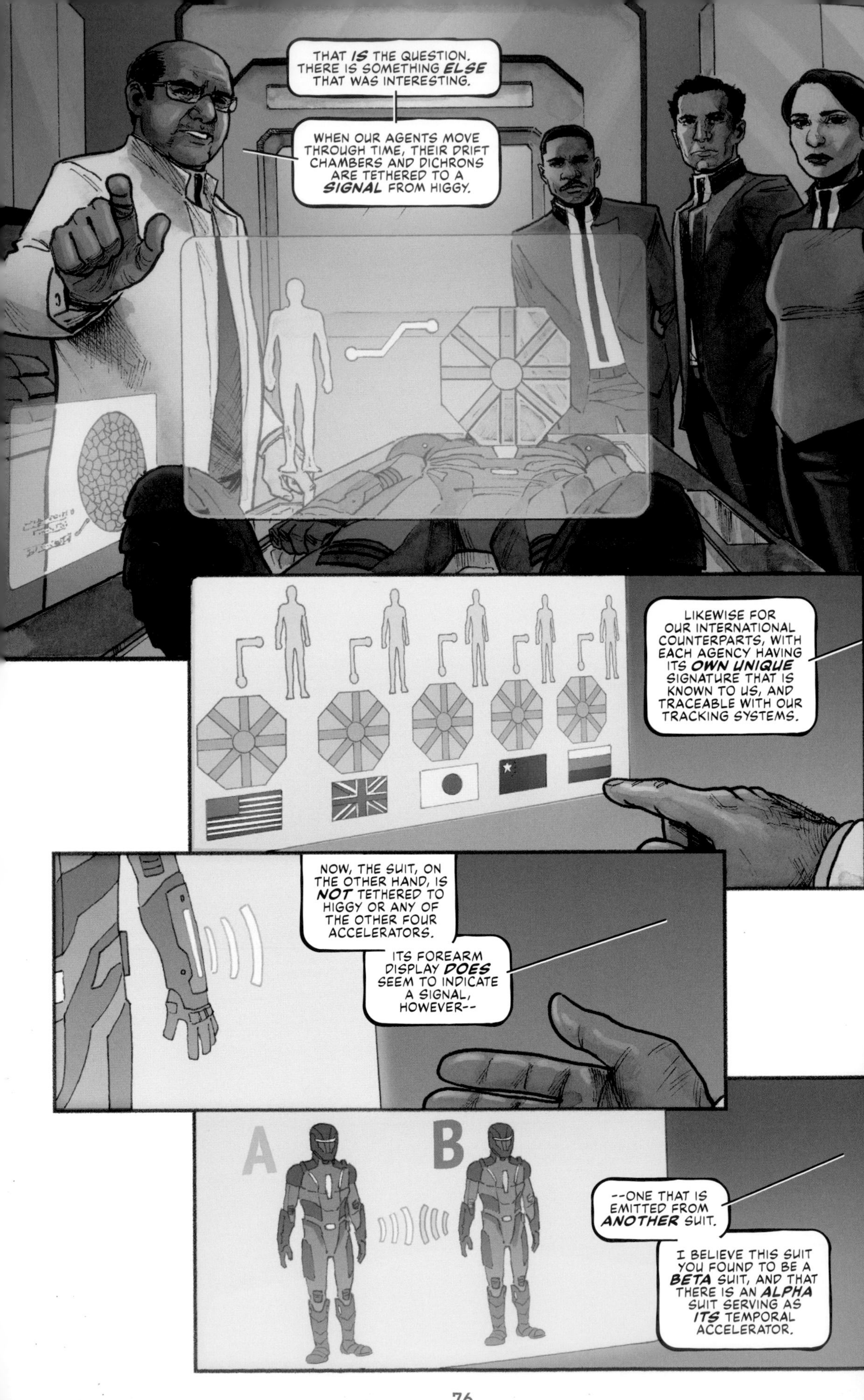
THAT IS THE QUESTION. THERE IS SOMETHING ELSE THAT WAS INTERESTING.
WHEN OUR AGENTS MOVE THROUGH TIME, THEIR DRIFT CHAMBERS AND DICHRONS ARE TETHERED TO A SIGNAL FROM HIGGY.
LIKEWISE FOR OUR INTERNATIONAL COUNTERPARTS, WITH EACH AGENCY HAVING ITS OWN UNIQUE SIGNATURE THAT IS KNOWN TO US, AND TRACEABLE WITH OUR TRACKING SYSTEMS.
NOW, THE SUIT, ON THE OTHER HAND, IS NOT TETHERED TO HIGGY OR ANY OF THE OTHER FOUR ACCELERATORS.
ITS FOREARM DISPLAY DOES SEEM TO INDICATE A SIGNAL, HOWEVER--
A
B
--ONE THAT IS EMITTED FROM ANOTHER SUIT.
I BELIEVE THIS SUIT YOU FOUND TO BE A BETA SUIT, AND THAT THERE IS AN ALPHA SUIT SERVING AS ITS TEMPORAL ACCELERATOR.

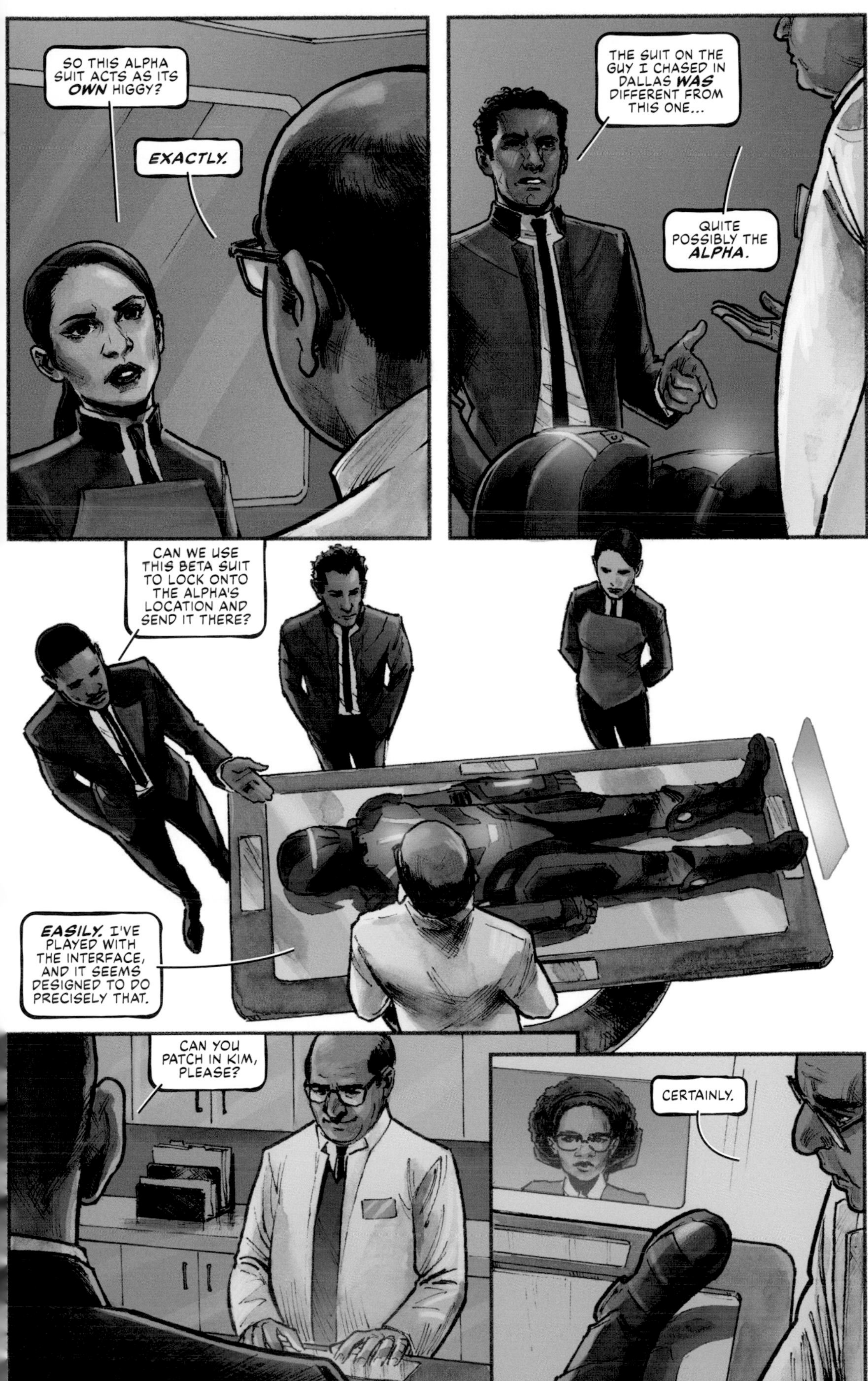
SO THIS ALPHA SUIT ACTS AS ITS OWN HIGGY?
EXACTLY.
THE SUIT ON THE GUY I CHASED IN DALLAS WAS DIFFERENT FROM THIS ONE...
QUITE POSSIBLY THE ALPHA.
CAN WE USE THIS BETA SUIT TO LOCK ONTO THE ALPHA'S LOCATION AND SEND IT THERE?
EASILY. I'VE PLAYED WITH THE INTERFACE, AND IT SEEMS DESIGNED TO DO PRECISELY THAT.
CAN YOU PATCH IN KIM, PLEASE?
CERTAINLY.

KIM, WHAT'S THE STATUS ON FIELD-TRACKING THE ANOMALIES?
WE'RE AT 90% CAPACITY OF ACTIVE AGENTS CURRENTLY PAIRED UP AND DEPLOYED, ATTEMPTING TO MAINTAIN CONTINUITY IN THE WAKE OF SEVERAL ANOMALY EVENTS, CHIEF.
AND THE ANOMALIES THEMSELVES?

THEIR SIGNALS ALL SEEM TO HAVE CONVERGED TO A CENTRAL POINT. LAMANAI, BELIZE. A REMOTE JUNGLE TEMPLE, FIVE YEARS BACK.
LAMANAI, BELIZE
THANK YOU.

YOU UP TO THIS? AGENT OLMOS IS CAPABLE, BUT I'M UNCOMFORTABLE THROWING HER INTO UNCHARTED WATERS THIS EARLY.
I CAN DO THIS, CHIEF.

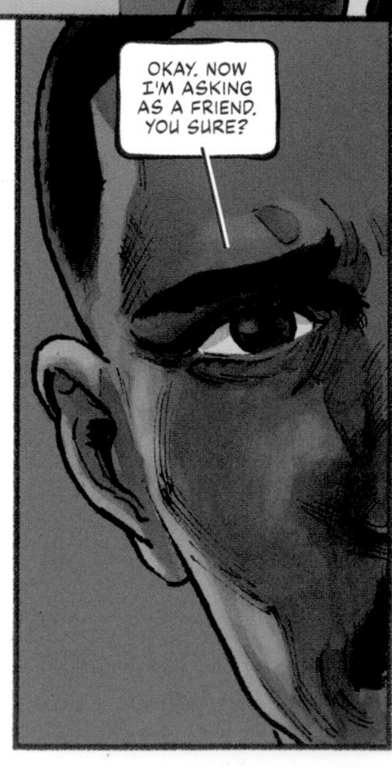
OKAY. NOW I'M ASKING AS A FRIEND. YOU SURE?

I'M SURE. THIS IS THE ONLY LEAD WE'VE HAD.
LET ME DO THIS, AVE.

OKAY.
SUIT UP.

NOW, 'RIK, YOU'LL BE ON YOUR OWN OUT THERE. WE'LL SEND AGENT OLMOS AND ANYONE ELSE WE CAN SPARE AS BACKUP TO THE NEAREST DRIFT LOCATION...

...BUT IT'LL STILL TAKE SOME TIME TO GET THEM CLOSE TO WHERE YOU'RE GOING.

YOU HAVE YOUR WEAPON AND DICHRON, CORRECT?

YES.

GOOD. WE'LL USE IT TO TRACK YOUR LOCATION AND VITALS.

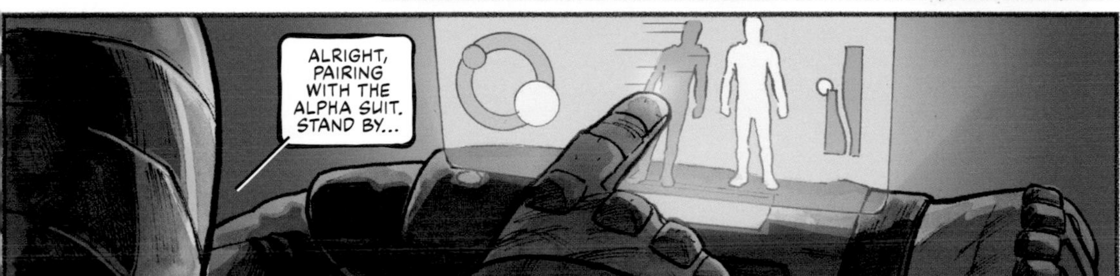

ALRIGHT, PAIRING WITH THE ALPHA SUIT. STAND BY...

THEN:
LAMANAI,
BELIZE.
2052.

THE ANCIENT MAYANS DEIFIED THE KEEPERS OF TIME.
THEY WERE CALLED "YEAR BEARERS."
GODS WHO WERE EACH ASSIGNED THEIR OWN MOUNTAINS AND WORSHIPPED ON A CYCLE AS THE BEARERS OF A NEW YEAR.

PRIESTS CALLED "DAYKEEPERS" WOULD PRAY TO THESE GODS OF TIME, SEEKING DIRECTION ON IMPORTANT DATES FOR THE PROSPERITY OF THEIR LANDS.

DO YOU KNOW WHAT HAPPENS WHEN THE SUBJECTS THEMSELVES BECOME GODS OF TIME, DECIDING THEIR OWN FATE?
WE FUCK EVERYTHING UP.

LET'S GO FOR A RIDE.

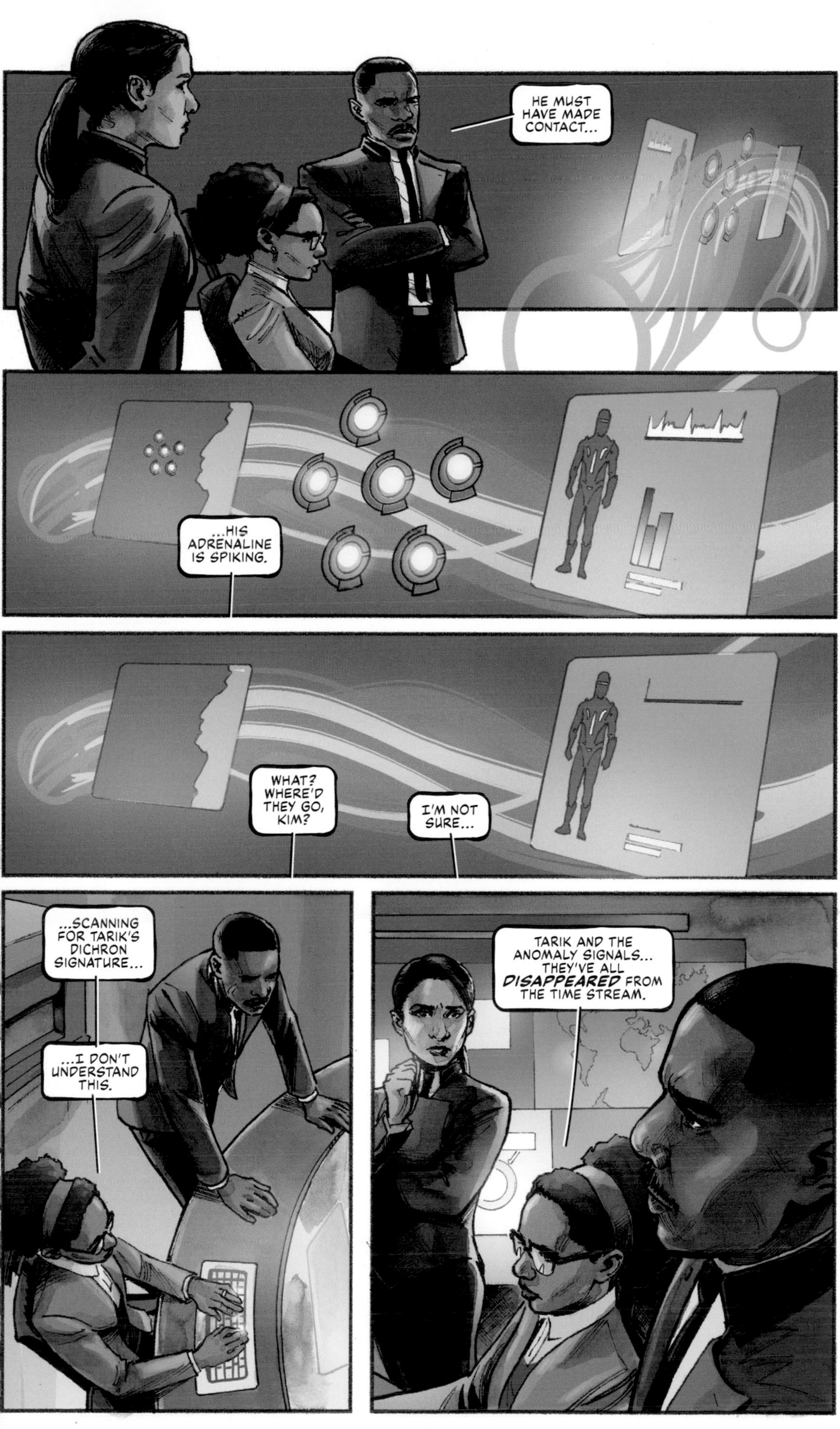

HE MUST HAVE MADE CONTACT...
...HIS ADRENALINE IS SPIKING.

WHAT? WHERE'D THEY GO, KIM?
I'M NOT SURE...

...SCANNING FOR TARIK'S DICHRON SIGNATURE...
...I DON'T UNDERSTAND THIS.

TARIK AND THE ANOMALY SIGNALS... THEY'VE ALL DISAPPEARED FROM THE TIME STREAM.

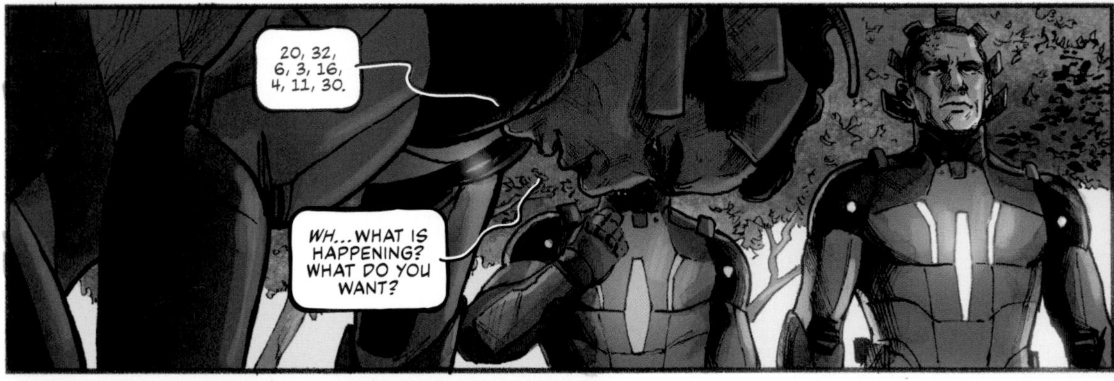

THINK OF US AS THE ***DAYKEEPERS.*** WE'RE HERE TO GIVE THE POWER OF TIME ***BACK*** TO THE GODS.

AND ***YOU'RE*** GOING TO HELP US.

THAT WAS ***YOU*** BACK IN DALLAS.

IT WAS.

"IS THAT WHY YOU LET ME LIVE? BECAUSE I'M *YOU?*"

"OF COURSE. IF *YOU* DIE, *I* DIE."

"DALLAS WAS A *MISDIRECT...*"

I NEED YOU SAFELY OUT OF THE WAY SO THAT WE CAN EXECUTE OUR OBJECTIVE.
IF THE BTA DISCOVERS IT'S ME WHO'S BEEN CAUSING ALL THE FUSS, IT'S YOU THAT THEY'LL GO AFTER IN ORDER TO STOP ME RETROACTIVELY.
I CAN'T HAVE THAT.
AND WHAT EXACTLY IS YOUR "OBJECTIVE"?
FIVE OF THE WORLD'S MOST POWERFUL GOVERNMENTS HAVE THEIR THUMBS ON THE SCALE OF FATE. MEDDLING IN THE PAST TO CHANGE THE FUTURE.
WE'RE HERE TO AMPUTATE.
TO RETURN THE WORLD TO HOW IT SHOULD HAVE ALWAYS BEEN--WHERE NO ONE HAS TO CHOOSE BETWEEN "MAINTAINING CONTINUITY" AND LETTING THOUSANDS DIE.
WE'RE GOING TO DESTROY ALL FIVE TEMPORAL ACCELERATORS, THEREBY ERADICATING THE ENTIRE TIME TRAVEL APPARATUS.
WHAT? NO. YOU--
THE BTA IS NECESSARY. WE STOP HISTORICAL INTERFERENCE. WE PRESERVE.
WE SAVE LIVES.
YOU'VE NEVER ASKED YOURSELF WHY THE BTA STOPS ONE TERROR ATTACK BUT ALLOWS ANOTHER TO HAPPEN. ENSURES IT, EVEN.

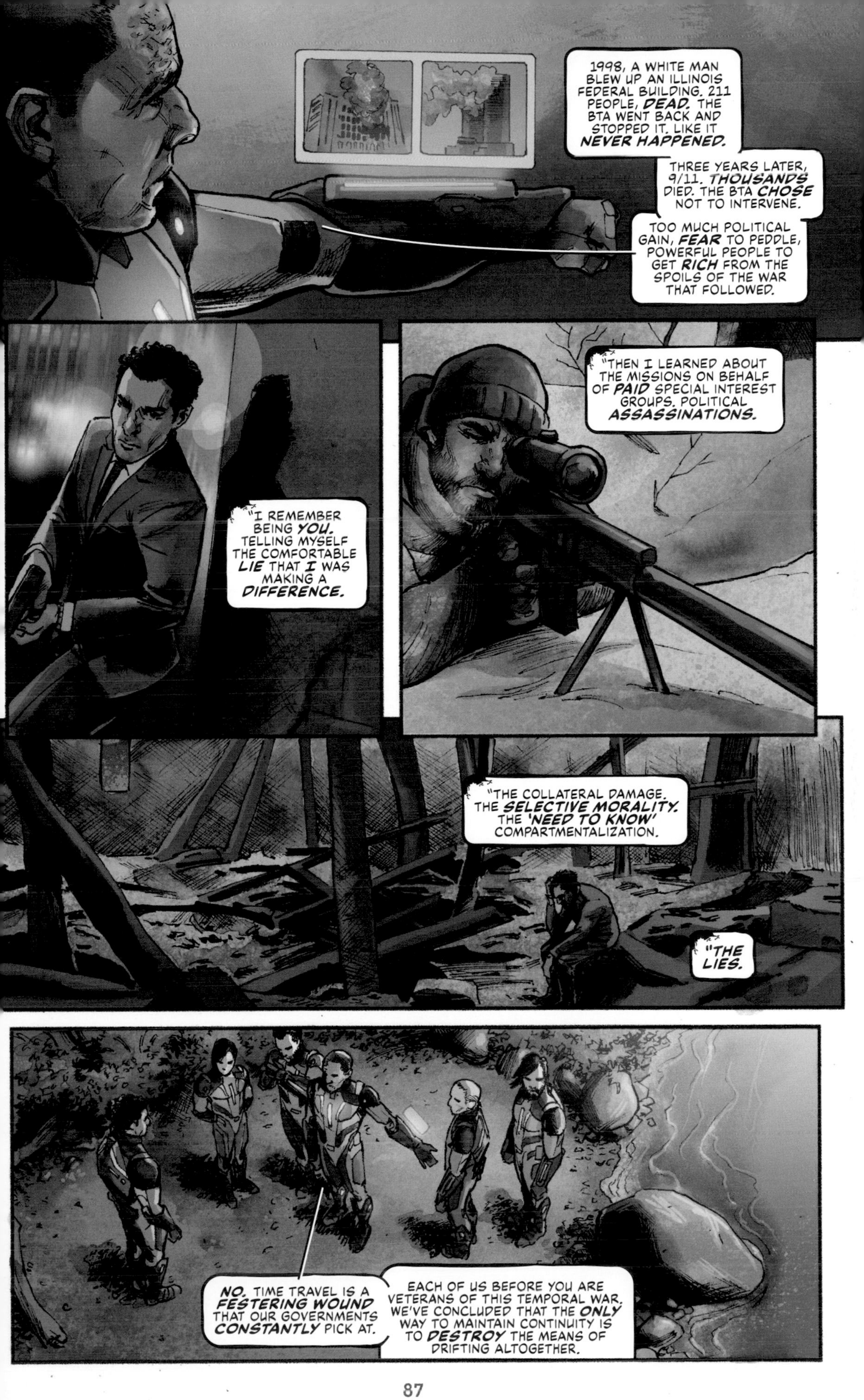

1998, A WHITE MAN BLEW UP AN ILLINOIS FEDERAL BUILDING. 211 PEOPLE, ***DEAD.*** THE BTA WENT BACK AND STOPPED IT. LIKE IT ***NEVER HAPPENED.***

THREE YEARS LATER, 9/11. ***THOUSANDS*** DIED. THE BTA ***CHOSE*** NOT TO INTERVENE.

TOO MUCH POLITICAL GAIN, ***FEAR*** TO PEDDLE, POWERFUL PEOPLE TO GET ***RICH*** FROM THE SPOILS OF THE WAR THAT FOLLOWED.

"I REMEMBER BEING ***YOU.*** TELLING MYSELF THE COMFORTABLE ***LIE*** THAT ***I*** WAS MAKING A ***DIFFERENCE.***

"THEN I LEARNED ABOUT THE MISSIONS ON BEHALF OF ***PAID*** SPECIAL INTEREST GROUPS. POLITICAL ***ASSASSINATIONS.***

"THE COLLATERAL DAMAGE. THE ***SELECTIVE MORALITY.*** THE ***'NEED TO KNOW'*** COMPARTMENTALIZATION.

"***THE LIES.***

THE BTA IS TRACKING ME-- AND WE'VE BEEN TRACKING YOU. THEY'LL COME FOR ME.
NOT HERE.
DO YOU RECOGNIZE THIS PLACE? I KNOW THE MISSION WAS BEFORE YOUR TIME.

THE HUDSON ENERGY CENTER. SOVEREIGNTY RADICALS FLY A PLANE INTO IT, FOUR HOURS FROM NOW. THEY'LL HIT ANOTHER TARGET 27 MINUTES LATER.
THE BTA STOPPED THOSE ATTACKS.
ONLY RETROACTIVELY. ONLY AFTER THEY HAD ALREADY TAKEN PLACE, LIKE SO MANY OF THE BTA'S EXERCISES IN BENEVOLENCE.
THIS ACTION CREATES A TIME REMNANT.
THESE REMNANTS ARE A FORK IN THE STREAM OF TIME, ITS FLOW DIVERTING INTO AN EDDY, FOREVER SWIRLING.
THE REMAINDER OF A TEMPORAL EQUATION THAT EXISTS OUTSIDE OF THE CONTINUITY OF TIME. AN INCOMPLETE CIRCUIT.
AND IT REPEATS ON A LOOP. OVER AND OVER AGAIN...

SO YOU SEE, YOUR DICHRON WON'T WORK HERE. JUST ANOTHER SECRET THE BTA HAS KEPT FROM YOU.
ANOTHER BIT OF THEIR COLLATERAL DAMAGE.

DO THEY KNOW? THE PEOPLE IN THE REMNANTS... DO THEY KNOW THEY'RE IN ONE?

NO. THEY'RE DOOMED TO DIE A FIERY AND VIOLENT DEATH IN THESE ATTACKS, EVERY DAY. THEIR SUFFERING IS ENDLESS.
AND THIS KIND OF REMNANT IS ONLY WHAT WE KNOW ABOUT. THERE COULD BE OTHERS. DIFFERENT FROM THIS. WORSE EVEN.

THIS IS WHY THE APPARATUS MUST BE DISMANTLED. WE'VE ALREADY DESTROYED THE TEMPORAL ACCELERATORS IN TOKYO, MOSCOW, BEIJING, AND LONDON--THREE DAYS FROM NOW.
ALL THAT'S LEFT IS "HIGGY" AT THE BTA.

WITH YOU SAFELY IN A REMNANT, I CAN WALK RIGHT INTO THE BTA WITH YOUR BIOMETRIC CLEARANCE AND RESTORE THE WORLD TO ITS PROPER STATE.
WAIT...

WHAT ABOUT THE AGENTS IN THE FIELD? IF YOU DESTROY THE ACCELERATORS, THEY'LL BE STUCK IN THE PAST. SOME OF THEM IN WAR ZONES...
...THE PEOPLE IN THE OFFICES, THE LABS... IF THAT ACCELERATOR BLOWS, EVERYONE INSIDE COULD BE INJURED OR KILLED.

THEY'VE ALL BEEN PARTY TO THE COLLATERAL DAMAGE. THEY KNEW THE RISKS WHEN THEY TOOK THE JOB.
REGARDLESS, ALL GREAT CHANGE REQUIRES GREAT SACRIFICE. THEIR DEATHS WILL NOT BE IN VAIN.

BUT...THE ACCELERATORS CAN BE REBUILT. THERE ARE BLUEPRINTS, SCHEMATICS... THE SCIENCE EXISTS.
NOT ANYMORE. WHY DO YOU THINK THE BTA HAS BEEN DETECTING OUR VARIOUS SIGNALS RECENTLY? WHAT DID THEY CALL US? "PEBBLES IN THE STREAM"?
AND YOUR SUITS? YOU'LL BE DESTROYING THEM AFTER YOUR MISSION, RIGHT?

YOU LET US WORRY ABOUT THAT.

OH, HOW RIGHTEOUS OF YOU. WILLING TO LET OTHERS DIE FOR YOUR CAUSE WHILE YOU DRIFT THROUGH TIME AND DECIDE THINGS FOR EVERYONE ELSE.
HOW ARE YOU ANY DIFFERENT THAN THE AGENCIES YOU DEFECTED FROM?

YOU **COWER** IN BATHROOMS WHILE YOU RECITE YOUR LITTLE NUMBERS SEQUENCE. YOU'LL START MIXING THEM UP AND YOU'LL BE **SCARED.** *"AM I LOSING IT?"*

AND THEN, ONE DAY, YOU'LL REALIZE THAT THOSE NUMBERS THAT WERE MEANT TO BE AN **ANCHOR** TO THE STREAM WERE **ACTUALLY** KEEPING YOU **BURIED** AT THE **BOTTOM** OF THE RIVER.

AND YOU'LL DECIDE TO **STOP** BEING WEAK AND WRITE YOUR **OWN** SEQUENCE IN **WHICHEVER** ORDER **YOU** PLEASE. AND WHEN THAT HAPPENS...

...YOU'LL BE READY TO SERVE A GREATER GOOD.

THEN:
MANHATTAN, 2048.

WE'LL BE BACK FOR YOU AT SOME POINT. WEEKS, MAYBE MONTHS TO YOU. TIME MOVES SLOWLY WHEN UNBURDENED BY CONTINUITY.

YOU'LL BE PLACED BACK IN YOUR OWN TIME WHEN WE'RE DONE, WHEN THERE IS NO MORE DRIFTING. NO OPPORTUNITY FOR...REPRISALS.
YOU'LL HAVE HAD PLENTY OF TIME TO RECONSIDER YOUR POSITION ON THE ETHICS OF TIME TRAVEL--AFTER BEING A PRISONER OF ITS REFUSE.

WHAT?
DAD WOULD BE ASHAMED OF YOU.

TAKE HIS SUIT.

NOW: MANHATTAN, 2048.
This is going to be my last loop. The anomalies-- my older-self-- they could return at any time.
This is it, I promise myself...
REEEE
WOOH
ROUGH NIGHT?
I have to get out of here before they can come back for me.
NYPD
My older-self called the remnant an "incomplete circuit" that exists outside of continuity.
If I can **prevent** these attacks and **complete** that circuit, it might reconnect the remnant to the time stream.
If it works, I'll be able to use my Dichron again and return to my own time.
I'll intercept the drift suit before Lucia takes it to the lab, and use it to get a jump on the Anomalies.
I need to stop them from killing anyone at the BTA or stranding agents in the past.

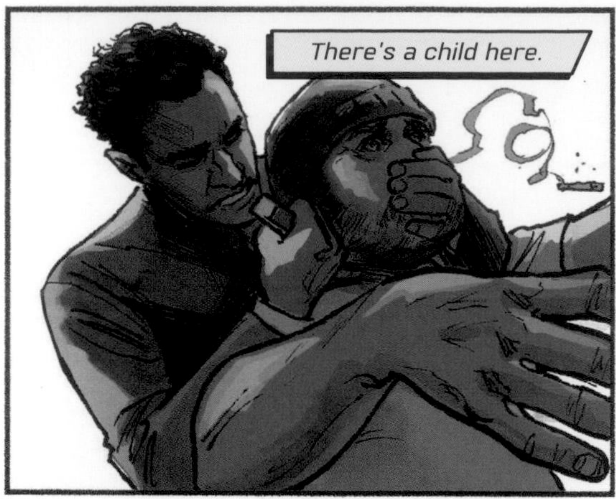
There's a child here.

I can't approach this like I did before.

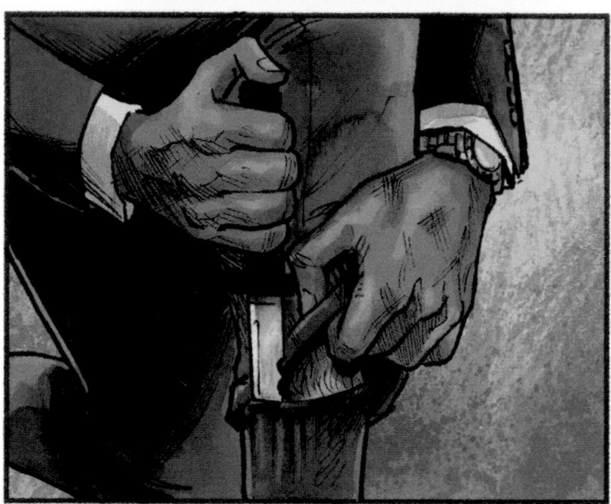

I was stuck in a sequence.

I have to change it up.
B-BOOM

BLAM
BLAM
BLAM
BLAM
BLAM
KRAK

Damnit. Another loop...

WAKE UP, YOU PIECE-A SHIT!

THAK

YOU KILLED MY FUCKIN' BROTHER!

Wait...no. Still here. In the barn.

Okay. This is... Good. This works. I can adapt.

Need to make sure the kid and her mother are safe.

YOU...YOU HAVE A BUNKER... UNDERGROUND.

HOW THE HELL DO YOU KNOW THAT?

DOESN'T MATTER.

THE WOMAN AND THE KID. PUT THEM DOWN THERE.

DON'T FUCKIN' TELL US WHAT TO DO, MOTHERF--

He doesn't know about my knife.
I'M NOT TELLING YOU SHIT.
But I know about the broken chair.
KRAK
HRGHHH!
GRRKK!

HRRRRRGH!
HGRR YOU FUCKER!
GRRK!
HNNG!
GYAH!
GKK!
GLLKKH!

Only one of them left now.

I need to take this whole armory down with him.

BLAM BLAM

AW SHIT!

HNG!

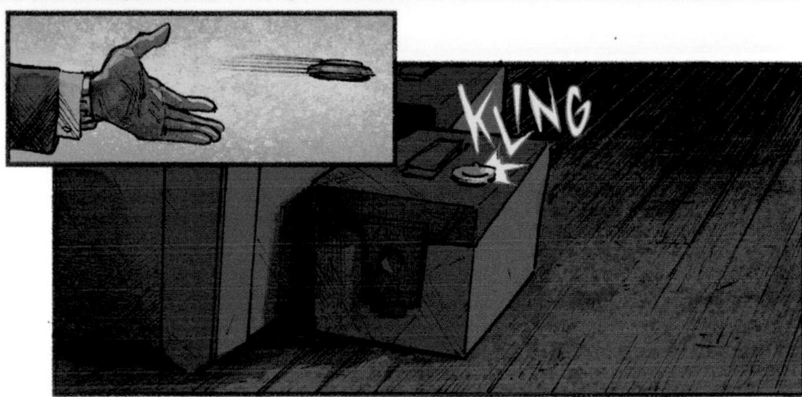

GYAH!

Their stockpiled ammo is set off by the flames.

BAM BAM BAM

Thank God. I did it.

I finally broke the--

YOU SONOFABITCH!

IS MY HUSBAND DEAD?!
PLEASE, JUST--
--JUST TAKE THE KID AND GO, OKAY?
TELL ME RIGHT NOW!
YOU CAN SAY YOU HAD NO IDEA WHAT THEY WERE PLANNING.
PLEASE, JUS--
CH-CHK
FUCK YOU, YOU FUCKIN' SAND NI--
BLAM

My Dichron is on again, which means they haven't destroyed Higgy yet. I should be able to make it home.
But I have to do something first...
She saw her mother die. She'll relive that moment for the rest of her life. Just like I've been reliving this day.
I tell myself the comfortable lie that I committed the lesser evil for the greater good.
But she's just another kind of remnant that exists because of me.
I wrote the coordinates of the compound on her shirt and dropped her at a hospital.
I made an anonymous call telling them she's an orphan. I instructed them to call the FBI and give them those coordinates so the Feds can find the answers they need.
I couldn't risk being detained for what happened at the compound. If I did this right, the day won't repeat again.
No more do-overs.
I find the nearest drift site...
...and I return to the moment after Lucia and I left for Dallas.

NOW: BTA HQ, MARYLAND. 2057.
I wondered if I'd ever see this place again. And now the sight of it makes me feel sick to my stomach.

My older-self was right. We're playing God here, and it hurts people.
I've hurt people.

But he and his compatriots are hypocrites.
They plan to keep their drift suits. They'll destroy the ability to time travel for everyone but themselves.

I can't let that happen.
I can't make right what I've done. But I can put a stop to the wrong.

I start by checking on Mom earlier in the day, like I should have.
CONTINUIT
Memory Care Fac

I haven't seen her in months, relative to my time in the remnant.
TARIK?
But she'll see my past-self later today when he comes to check on her after the Dallas mission.
AYWA, MOM.
HABIBI, WHAT HAPPENED TO YOUR FACE?
It's the first time she's recognized me in a long while.
It's bittersweet, because I barely recognize myself.
What was it that he said to me?
"Eventually, you'll start mixing them up and you'll be scared... Am I going crazy?"
That I would "decide to stop being weak" and write my own sequence.
That's exactly what I'm going to do...
GOODBYE, MOM. I LOVE YOU.

My past-self and Lucia will be returning from Dallas any second.

I need to get that case from her after they part ways.

She was really unhappy with me in this moment.

This won't be easy.

LUCIA, WAIT!

ON SECOND THOUGHT, I SHOULD PROBABLY TAKE THIS IN.
THEY CAN BE STICKLERS ABOUT CHAIN OF CUSTODY STUFF WITH EVIDENCE...
WHAT HAPPENED TO YOUR FACE?
OH...I--OPEN LOCKER DOOR IN THE LOCKER ROOM--WALKED RIGHT INTO IT.
YOU WALKED ALL THE WAY TO THE LOCKER ROOM AND BACK JUST NOW? AND BANDAGED YOURSELF?

YEAH I WAS IN A HURRY. LOOK IT'S NOT A BIG DEAL, I'LL JUST--
THE HELL IS GOING ON?
She's not buying this. I'm going to have to level with her.

OKAY, LOOK... I'M ON A MISSION, AND I NEED YOUR HELP.
I KNOW YOU DON'T TRUST ME YET. AND YOU'RE ABOUT TO GO TELL AVERY THAT I WAS RECKLESS IN DALLAS.
AND YOU'RE RIGHT TO DO SO. I WAS.

BUT I NEED YOU TO TRUST ME NOW.

THE ANOMALIES, DALLAS... THERE'S A SERIES OF EVENTS IN MOTION THAT I NEED TO STOP, AND I NEED THAT CASE TO DO IT.
YOU HAVE TO GO TO AVERY AND TELL HIM TO INITIATE RECALL.
BRING IN ALL OF THE AGENTS IN THE FIELD? WHY?
THERE'S GOING TO BE AN ATTACK HERE AT HQ. IT COULD LEAVE ACTIVE AGENTS STRANDED IN THE PAST AND KILL EVERYONE INSIDE THIS BUILDING.
NO. YOU'RE NOT PULLING THIS LONE WOLF SHIT AGAIN.
IF THIS IS WHAT YOU SAY IT IS, THEN YOU'RE GOING TO NEED TO TRUST ME TO HELP YOU. WE RUN THIS LIKE AN OP.
YOU'RE RIGHT: LIKE AN OP.
GOOD. I'LL MAKE SURE I'M ON COMMS. TELL ME WHAT YOU NEED US TO DO.
THANK YOU, LUCIA.

My older self is too far gone. His quest to put an end to collateral damage and suffering will only create more.

When all is said and done, if he gets his way, more people will die, and time travel will still exist. But on **his** terms.

"Lone wolf shit," as Lucia put it.

That cannot stand.

In order to destroy the apparatus, it **all** has to go. The Accelerators, Higgy, the drift suits. **All of it.**

I make one last stop...

NOW:
BTA DRIFT SITE,
PHILADELPHIA.
2042.
...to say goodbye.

NOW: LAMANAI, BELIZE. 2052.

*This time I surprise **them**.*

LET'S GO SEE HIM.

NO TASERS THIS TIME.
I'M HERE BECAUSE I WANT TO BE. YOU DON'T HAVE TO TRY AND TRAP ME IN THE REMNANT. THAT ALREADY HAPPENED.
YOU--YOU ESCAPED IT? HOW?

THAT'S NOT IMPORTANT.
WHAT MATTERS IS THAT I'VE HAD...TIME... TO RECONSIDER MY THOUGHTS ON THE ETHICS OF TIME TRAVEL.
AND I THINK YOU'RE RIGHT.
THE APPARATUS NEEDS TO BE DESTROYED.
A comfortable lie. I guess I'm still telling them to myself, in some form.

I'M GOING TO HELP YOU.
NIET. HE'S NOT COMING WITH US. WE DON'T NEED HIM FOR THIS, IT'S A FIVE-MAN JOB. HE'S--

NOW WE'RE FIVE.
YOU SONOFA BITCH!
NO.
YOU TOLD ME I WOULD STOP BEING WEAK AND START WRITING MY OWN SEQUENCE.
I'M COMING WITH YOU.

GOOD WORK, AGENT OLMOS.

KIM! WE'VE GOT A SITUATION-- I'M INITIATING RECALL. I NEED SIT-REPS ON EVERY ACTIVE AGENT IN THE FIELD...

EVERYONE ELSE! OUT OF THE BUILDING!

THIS IS NOT A DRILL!

RECALL

CHIEF, WE CURRENTLY HAVE **SEVENTEEN ACTIVE AGENTS** IN THE FIELD.
EYES UP, EVERYONE...

"...THEY'RE *HERE.*"

Their plan is simple: 3 explosive charges placed on Higgy. Both ends, and at the center.

Once armed, we'll have 30 seconds before detonation.

My older-self will override our suits and drift us all to a nearby rendezvous point, where we can watch the fall of the empire in all of its glory.

Then they use my suit to drop me back into my own continuity. Right after I left for Belize the first time, later today.

And they go do whatever they want, skipping through time at their leisure. A "pension" for their years of service.

But I threw a wrench into their gears.

HE *WARNED* THEM.

RECALL?

TAKARA, BRANDT, GO AND BLOW THE DRIFT CHAMBERS WHILE WE PLANT OUR CHARGES. TAKE OUT ANYONE THAT GETS IN YOUR WAY.

BLOWING THE
DRIFT CHAMBERS
WASN'T PART
OF THE PLAN!
NEITHER WAS
WARNING EVERYONE
THAT WE WERE
COMING. WE CAN'T
RISK AGENTS
COMING BACK TO
SABOTAGE
OUR MISSION.

I TOLD YOU
THERE WOULD
BE SACRIFICES.
YOU'VE FORCED
MY HAND.

ZHAO, PLANT YOUR
CHARGE ON THE FAR
END. MY COUNTERPART
AND I WILL HANDLE THE
MAIN ACCELERATOR
HOUSING AND THE
CENTRAL CHANNEL.

JESUS... THEY'RE
GOING TO BLOW THE
ACCELERATOR.
HOW MANY
AGENTS ARE
STILL IN THE
FIELD?
TOO MANY.
LUCIA.
TARIK. GO
AHEAD...

THEY'RE GOING FOR THE DRIFT CHAMBERS...
...YOU'VE GOTTA STOP THEM BEFORE THEY GET THERE.
THEY'RE GOING TO BLOW THE DRIFT CHAMBERS!

BLAM
BLAM

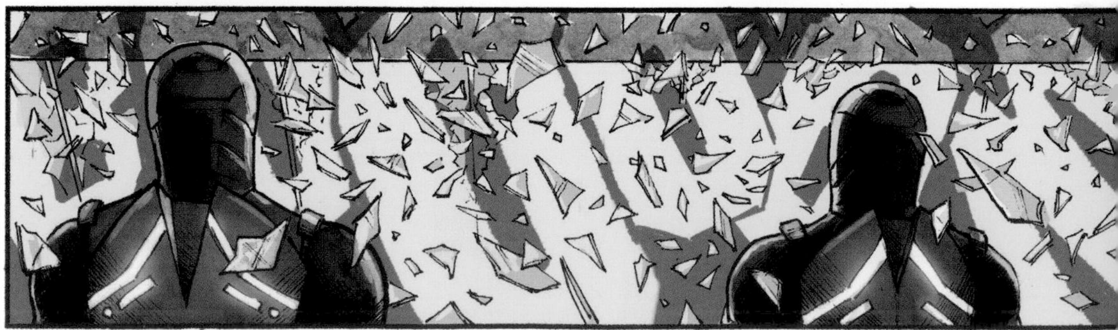

BLAM
BLAM

THEY'RE SETTING THE CHARGE!
BLAM
GYAH!
BLAM

DAMNIT! IT'S BEEN SHOT!

NNNNN...

PULL HIM CLEAR!

LUCIA--

GO!

HNNNGG!

...THIS PLACE IS ABOUT TO BLOW.

TAKARA AND BRANDT ARE DEAD.
SHIT! THIS IS HIS FAULT!

AND THEN THERE WERE TWO...

WH--?
ALL GREAT CHANGE REQUIRES SACRIFICE.
I COULDN'T TRUST THEM WITH THE POWER THESE SUITS WOULD GIVE THEM.
HRRRGGHH!
'RIK, WE'RE THE LAST ONES INSIDE, AND WE'RE ABOUT TO GET CLEAR OF THE BUILDING...

"...DO WHAT YOU GOTTA DO, AND THEN GET THE HELL OUT OF THERE."
FINALLY...
...FOR THE GREATER GOOD.
ARM 00:30
As I watch the man before me, I think about who I was when this day started... An idealist.
I consider the path that led me here-- the time in the remnant-- how it changed me.
How it turned me into him.
And I realize... it's too late for me.
But if there's no him, and no me to become...
...then maybe that idealist from this morning who is visiting his mom right now still has a fighting chance at being better than both of us...

Unable to unknowingly cause more collateral damage.
EVERYONE GET BACK! GET CLEAR!
00:22

00:20
No more remnants.
DEET

00:18

00:17
KLING

00:16

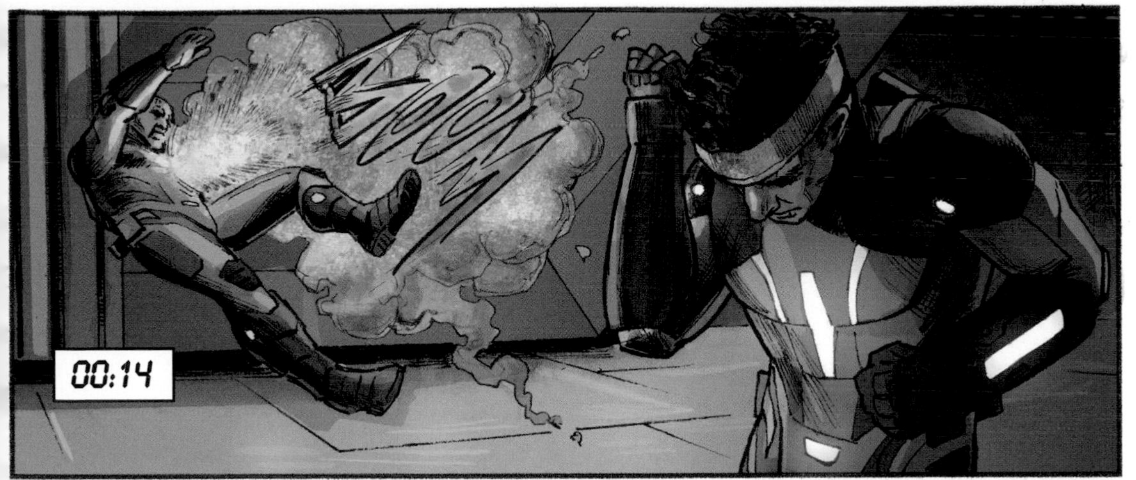
WOOOM
00:14

00:08
WH-- KOFF WHAT THE HELL ARE YOU DOING?!

00:04
WRITING MY OWN SEQUENCE.

00:01

"DO THEY KNOW? THE PEOPLE IN THE REMNANTS... DO THEY KNOW THEY'RE *IN* ONE?"

"NO. THEY'RE DOOMED TO DIE A *FIERY* AND *VIOLENT* DEATH IN THESE ATTACKS *EVERY DAY.* THEIR SUFFERING IS ENDLESS.
"AND THIS *KIND* OF REMNANT IS ONLY WHAT WE KNOW ABOUT. THERE COULD BE OTHERS. DIFFERENT FROM THIS. *WORSE,* EVEN..."

NOW: MARYLAND, 2057.
5:59AM

6:00AM

0600
SNOOZE

NEW VOICEMAIL:
DEENA

"MOM FELL AGAIN IN THE MIDDLE OF THE NIGHT. THEY **TRIED** CALLING YOU...YOU **NEED** TO GET OVER THERE ASAP, AND **CALL ME BACK.**"

SHIT.

RETROACTIVE

RETROSPECTIVE

A behind-the-scenes look at the making of *RetroActive*.

Ibrahim's design for Bureau of Temporal Affairs Agent Tarik Abdelnassar.

Ibrahim's design for Tarik's future self.

Ibrahim's designs for Agent Lucia Olmos and the dichron device each agent is equipped with.

Ibrahim's design for Special Agent in Charge Avery Woodard and the Bureau of Temporal Affairs logo.

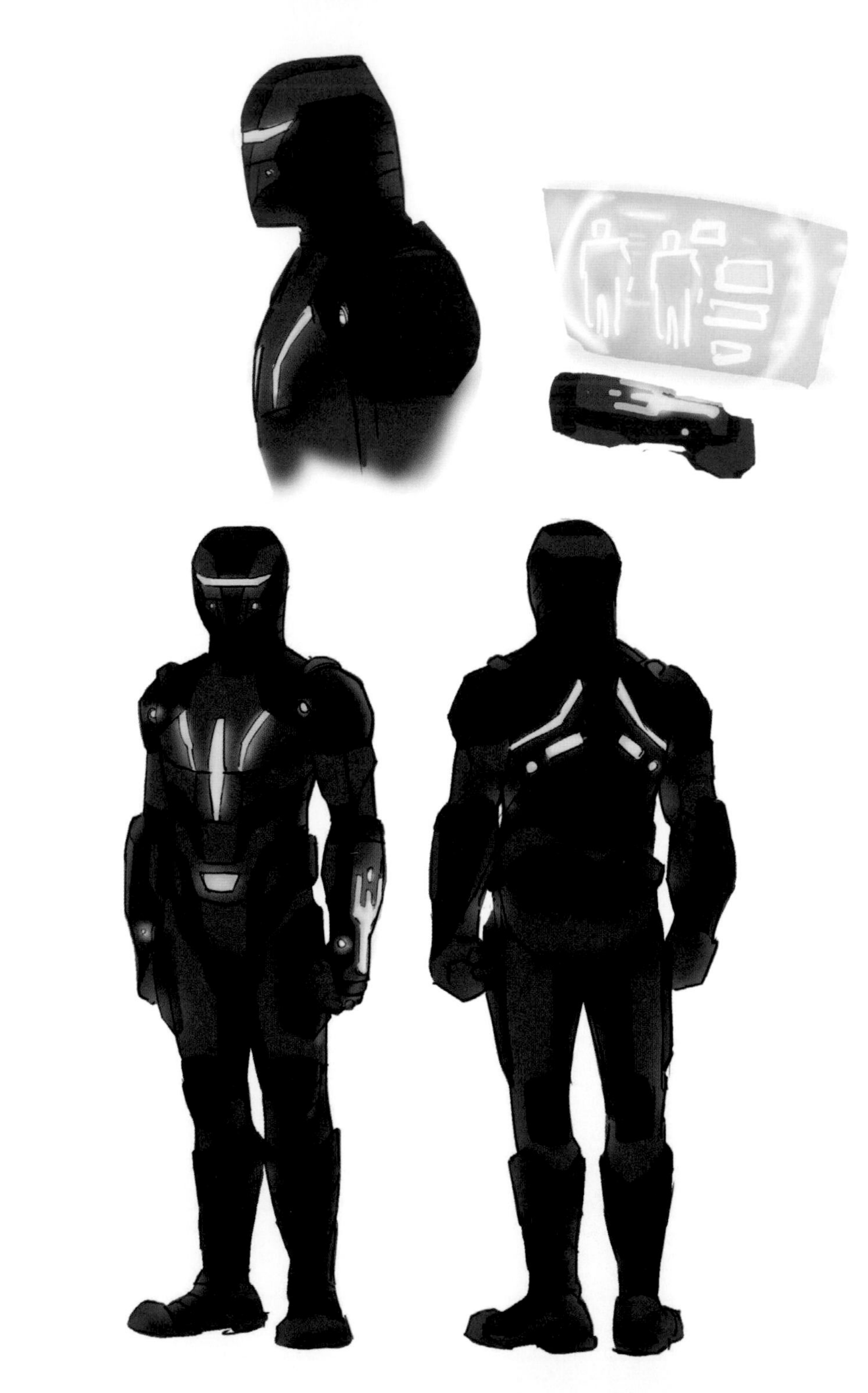

Ibrahim's design for the drift suits worn by future Tarik and his team.

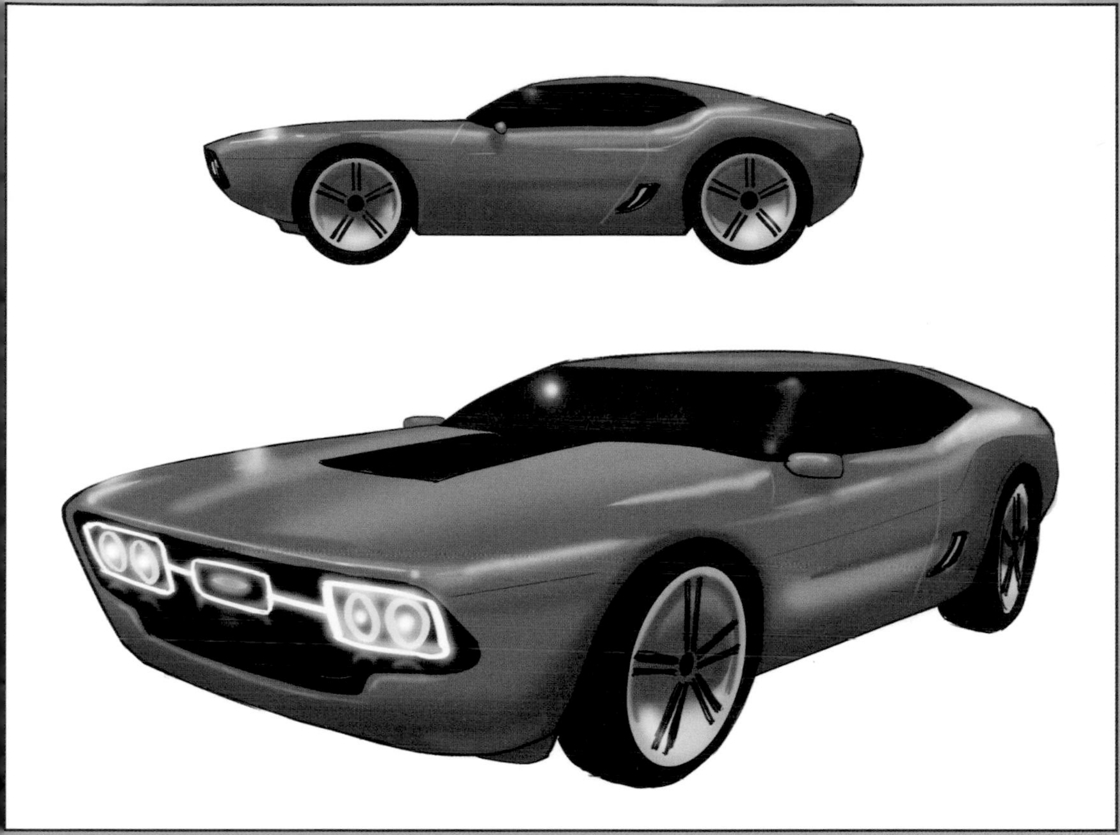

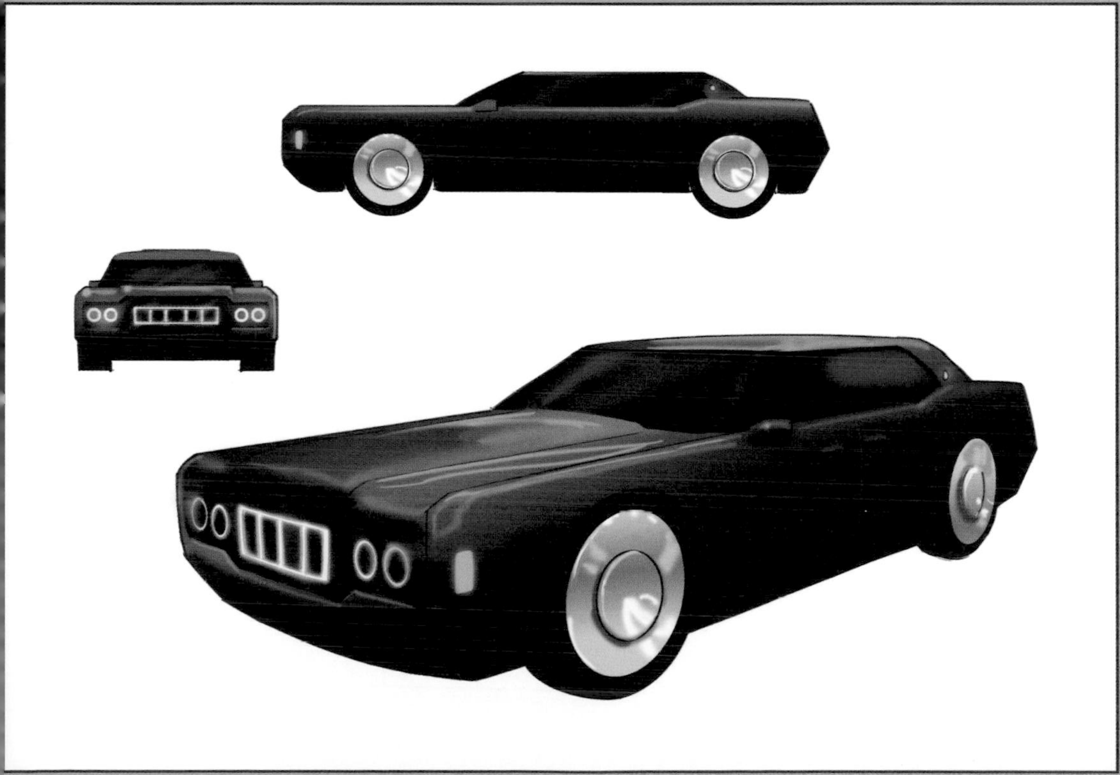

Ibrahim's design for the car Tarik drives in the present (top) and the sedan he steals in the time loop (bottom).

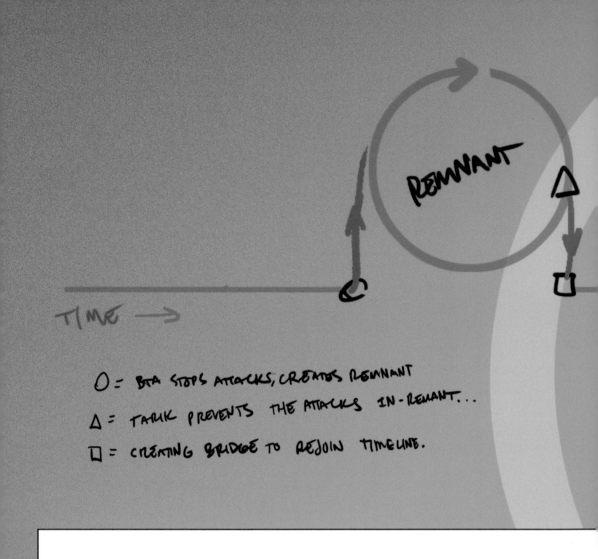

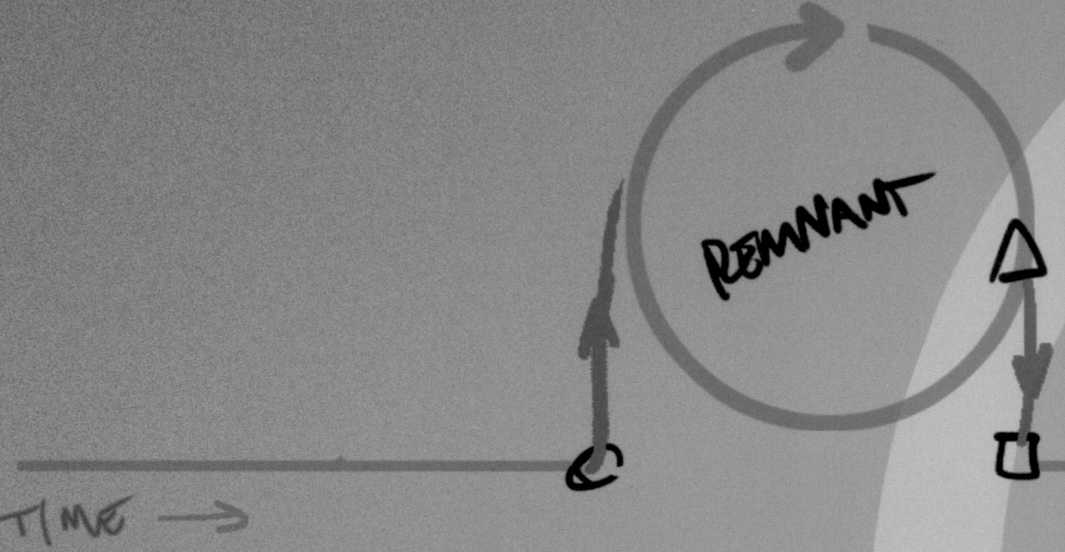

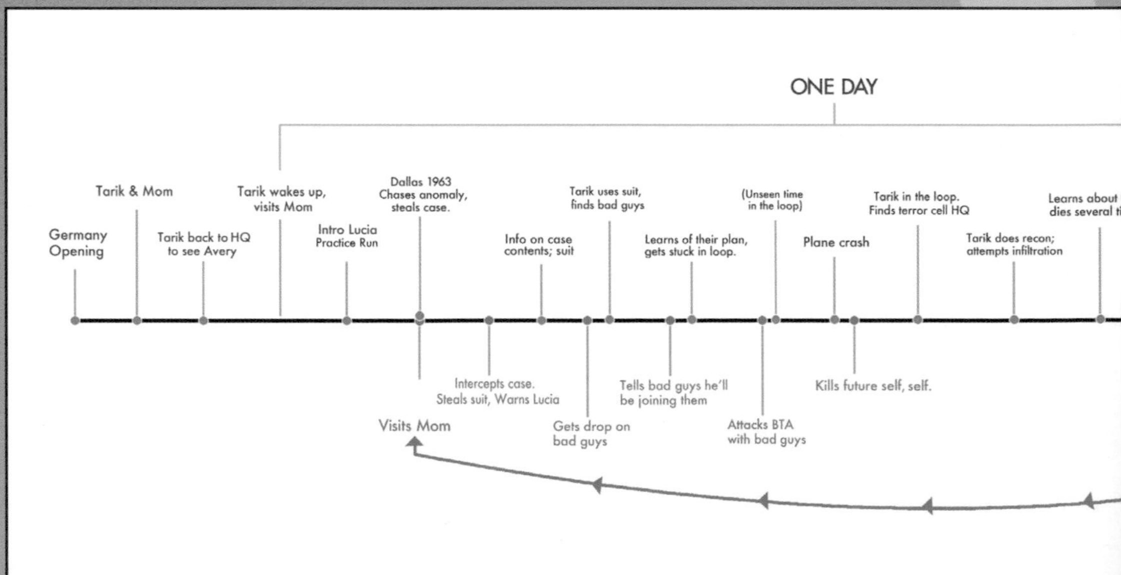

A time travel story like this can be a tough one to track and wrap your head around, so Ibrahim tracked the logic of both the remnant and the overall timeline to ensure that the internal logic of *RetroActive* actually made sense.

ass in the loop >
nects the timeline

Finds drift site,
goes back to present.

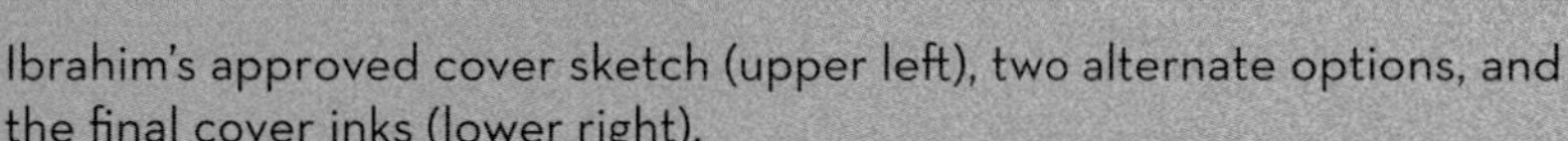

Ibrahim's approved cover sketch (upper left), two alternate options, and the final cover inks (lower right).

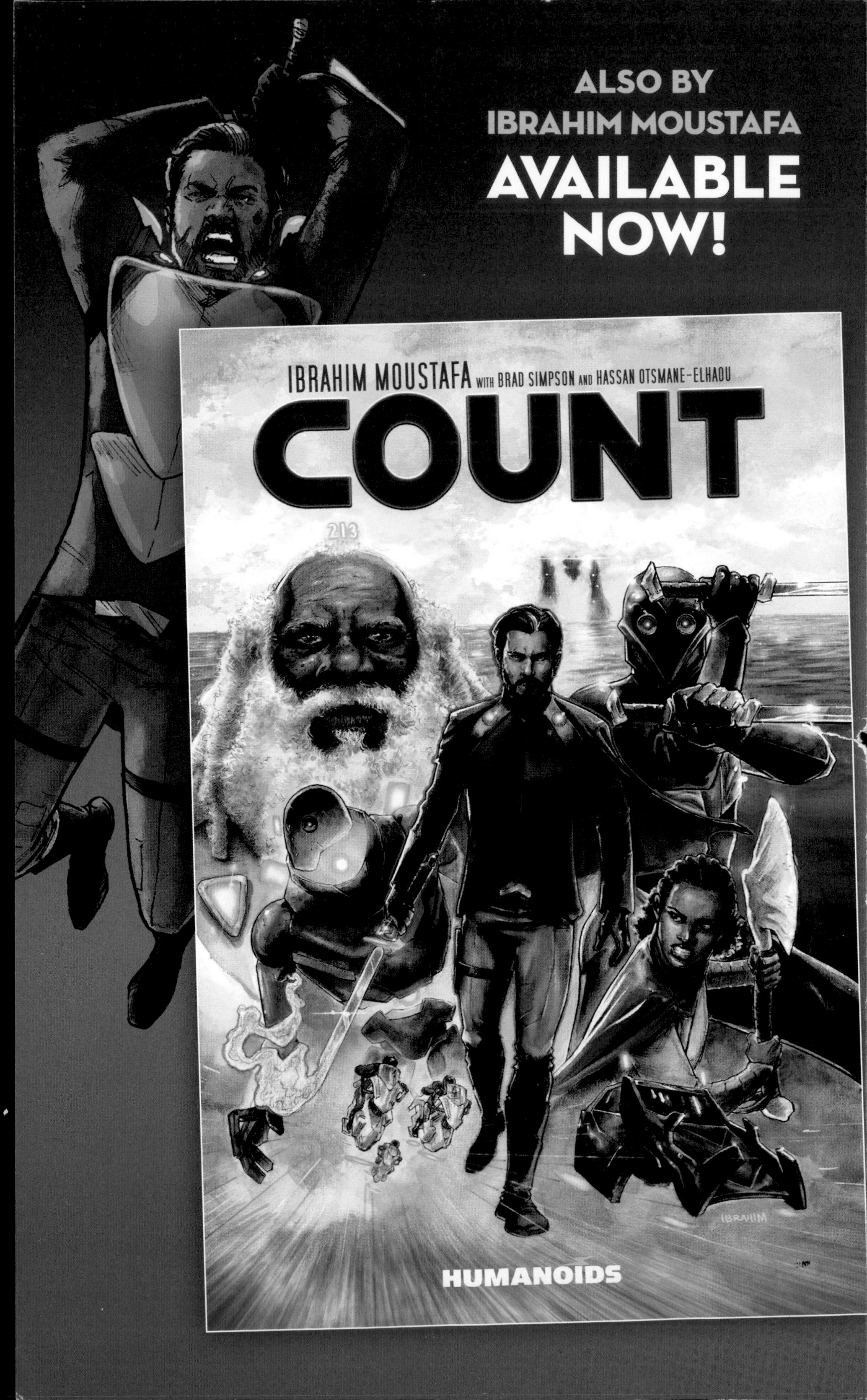

ALSO BY
IBRAHIM MOUSTAFA
AVAILABLE
NOW!